From PROJECT to PRODUCT MODE

A Game Plan to Unlock Scalability for B2B Software Products

This book is intentionally short.

It's easy to make simple things sound complicated.
It's hard to make complex problems sound simple.

Shifting your company from project to product is a very complex task.

Understanding the big picture is the key to making it solvable.

Our goal is to give you that clarity, so you can start transforming your organization into a scalable product company.

And we believe 2–3 hours of focused reading might be all it takes to get started.

"Many people talk about the shift from project to product – Sebastian and Thomas describe how it really works and how they really succeeded! This book is pure experience. Anyone struggling with structural boundaries as a product leader in a B2B setup will find the right language, a systematic approach, and a few words of encouragement here."

– Petra Wille, Product Coach, Author of STRONG Product People and STRONG Product Communities

"I wish I had read "From Project to Product Mode" years ago. It would have saved me (and my teams) a lot of pain. This book is clear, practical, and painfully accurate about the challenges of scaling B2B software. If you've ever felt stuck between delivering what sales promised and building what the product really needs, this book is for you. It gives language to the struggles, and – more importantly – a path forward."

– Joaquim Torres (Joca), Product Advisor & Author of Digital Transformation and Product Culture

"If you're serious about getting your company from juggling projects to real product growth, this book will save you years of pain. It is practical, brutally accurate, and focused on what actually scales. Read it. Be bold enough to act while others hide behind the status quo."

– David Pereira, Author of Untrapping Product Teams

“An essential guide for anyone leading the shift from a project to a product mindset. It will help you anticipate the challenges ahead and equip you with the actionable insights you need to overcome them. It's what every transformation superhero keeps on their night stand.”

- Radhika Dutt, Product Leader & Author of Radical Product Thinking: The New Mindset for Innovating Smarter

“I ran a B2B startup from 2014 to 2019. This book mirrors exactly how we scaled—stacking early projects into one product, segmenting hard, and only building what customers would pay for. It’s spot on.”

- Paweł Huryn, Founder and Author @The Product Compass

"Most product books tell you what to do. This one shows you why your company is stuck. Sebastian and Thomas nail the real problem: it's not just product teams that need to change—it's the entire system. The seven challenges framework is like having a diagnostic tool for organizational dysfunction. Essential reading for any product leader trying to break free from the feature factory trap."

— Ash Maurya, Author of Running Lean and Creator of Lean Canvas

PREFACE

Why and for Whom Is This Book

This book wasn't born in theory, it came from real-world practice.

Some years ago, while working closely with a client in the midst of a transformation, we started noticing the same patterns we had seen before: constant firefighting, bloated backlogs, overpromised roadmaps, and frustrated teams. To make sense of what was really going wrong, we sat down, talked to all the executives and mapped out the core struggles we saw, not just in this company, but in others we had worked with too.

That exercise became a turning point. It led us to identify the seven systemic challenges that almost every organization faces when shifting from project mode to product mode.

Since then, we've used this mental model with countless clients across different industries. Again and again, it has helped product leaders make sense of their organizational struggles. Therefore, it gave clarity and direction on how to act effectively.

We've seen these seven challenges resonate deeply with product managers, engineers, executives, and founders. And we believe they offer a shared language to spark alignment, change outdated habits, and focus the organization on what really matters to become a scalable product company...

This book is our way of putting that mental model and everything we've learned into the world. If you're on the path from project to product, we hope it becomes your companion, a tool to spark the right conversations, shift mindsets, and help you lead with clarity and conviction.

Who This Book Is For

This book is for product leaders in B2B software companies driving the transformation from project to product.

If you're a VP of Product, Head of Product, or CPO, you already know that product management isn't just about building great features, it's about changing how the entire company thinks about building products.

But what happens when you're in an organization that still operates in project mode? You likely will know these symptoms:

- Your company sells features, not solutions, creating endless custom work. Engineering capacity is consumed by one-off requests. Product complexity increases.
- Your engineering team is overwhelmed, constantly reacting instead of innovating. Technical debt grows. Morale drops. Important roadmap items get delayed.
- Your executives don't think in product strategy, they expect you to execute on stakeholder demands. Product becomes reactive. Teams lack focus. Short-term firefighting replaces long-term vision.
- Your roadmap is dictated by the biggest customers, not by a clear product vision. Growth slows. Smaller but more scalable opportunities are neglected. The product becomes a patchwork of exceptions.

Sound familiar? You're not alone. Many software companies, especially in the B2B and SaaS spaces, start out providing custom project work.

Eventually, they reach a point where they realize they need to scale. The challenge is that most organizations aren't sure how to shift from a project-driven approach to a truly scalable product mode.

What This Book Helps You Achieve

This book is here to help you lead that transformation. It is not just a theoretical book about project mode vs. product mode. This is your playbook for leading change as a product leader. Inside, you'll learn:

✔ Why your company is struggling to scale and how to fix it: Understand the core reasons why project-based thinking limits growth.

✔ How to regain control of your product: Shift from reacting to sales-driven demands to executing a real product strategy.

✔ How to align executives, from sales, marketing, finance, product, operations, and engineering: Change the mindset of your leadership team to think in terms of product success, not custom work.

✔ How to transition your company from project mode to a scalable product company: Get a framework for building a company that balances customer needs and business scalability.

✔ How to avoid common mistakes in the transformation: Learn the pitfalls that slow down or completely derail companies moving from project-based to product-based operations.

This book provides a mental framework that helps you move from firefighting to leading a successful, scalable product company.

Who This Book Is Not For

It's not a beginner's guide to product management fundamentals. Instead, it's written specifically for Product Leaders who already understand product management and are now tasked with driving organizational change. The focus in this book is the big picture of changing your organization.

If you're leading a team or an entire department, and you're frustrated by the lack of product thinking in your organization, this book will give you the strategies, frameworks, and tools to turn things around.

While it's primarily written for B2B organizations with complex software products.

B2C companies may recognize similar patterns, especially those where stakeholders prescribe solutions instead of defining outcomes. In those cases, simply replace "customer" with "stakeholder" or "management," and you'll likely be surprised how well it still fits.

How This Book Is Structured

This book follows the typical journey of a Product Leader who needs to transition their company from a project mindset to a product mindset:

Chapter 1: Understanding the Problem
Why project companies struggle and how to recognize if you're in one.

Chapter 2: The 7 Biggest Challenges in the Transition
The key roadblocks you'll face and how to overcome them.

Chapter 3: Leading the Change
A structured approach to shifting your company toward product-driven success.

Chapter 4: Common Misconceptions
The hidden beliefs that quietly derail your transformation...

Get Ready to Lead the Change

Your role as a Product Leader is more than just building products, it's about building the right environment to support product thinking. If you're stuck in an organization that operates like a feature factory, this book is your guide to making the shift happen.

CHAPTER 1

Differences Between Project Mode and Product Mode

To understand how companies move from a project-oriented organization to a product-driven one, it helps to first trace how many of them begin.

How Many B2B Software Companies Start Off

Software products in the B2B world often begin with a single customer need. A project is launched to solve that specific challenge. After successful implementation, the question arises: could we sell this solution to others?

Examples of Products That Started as Projects

- **Basecamp** was developed by a web design firm for its internal needs before it became a standalone tool.[1] [2]
- **Shopify** was originally an internal tool to sell snowboards online. When the founders realized others had similar needs, they turned it into a product.[3] [4]
- **SAP** began by digitizing payroll at a German IBM subsidiary. Its success led to the founding of SAP as a software company.[5]

---

[1] Ryan Singer, Shape Up, https://basecamp.com/shapeup/0.3-chapter-01. Accessed 25.04.2025.

[2] From Jason Fried's Medium Blog: https://medium.com/%40jasonfried/basecamp-the-origin-story-f509fdd725f8. Accessed 25.04.2025.

[3]https://producthabits.com/shopify-grew-snowboard-shop-10b-commerce-ecosystem/. Accessed 25.04.2025. Accessed 25.04.2025.

[4] Watch the Shopify Origin Story here: https://youtu.be/6-HsPMTQ19c. Accessed 25.04.2025.

[5] https://en.wikipedia.org/wiki/SAP. Accessed 25.04.2025.

In each case, a project became a product. What started as a one-off solution was generalized to serve others.

Growth Through Project Stacking

After the successful first project, the team starts to look for further customers. New customers join one after another. As success builds, the company begins to grow. More customers come on board, each with slightly different needs. To close the deals, the company agrees to implement custom features:

- One customer wants an extra field.
- Another asks for a new report.
- A third needs integration with a special internal tool.
- The next customer wants a whole new module.

At first, these additions seem manageable. But customer by customer, the product turns into a growing collection of special cases. We call this **project stacking**: layering one-off solutions on top of one another.

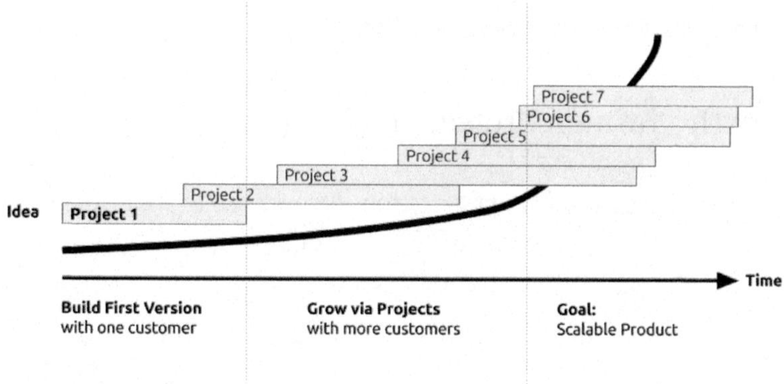

The team is proud of its success. The company grows quickly, some companies we saw sprinted to 100 employees and millions in revenue within a couple of years. But the software becomes harder to maintain. Releases break things. Testing becomes unpredictable. The code is full of edge cases, resulting from the noble intention to solve problems for individual customers, the product fails to solve them well...

Every customer implementation becomes a new project, and engineering is in permanent crisis mode.

The Tipping Point

Eventually, complexity overwhelms the organization. Development output slows. Promises aren't met. Sales sells features that can't be built or delivered on time. Engineering delivers hotfixes and bug fixes just to keep customers satisfied. Different customers run different versions of the product.

Tension builds across departments. Sales blames engineering. Engineering blames sales. Product management, if it exists, is caught in the middle, trying to translate unfiltered requests into something the team can build.

Leadership grows frustrated. "We were faster with 10 people than we are now with 100." It becomes hard, if not impossible, to plan and the expected growth prediction cannot be achieved.

This is the point at which many companies realize something must change. They start to think: maybe we need to become a product company.

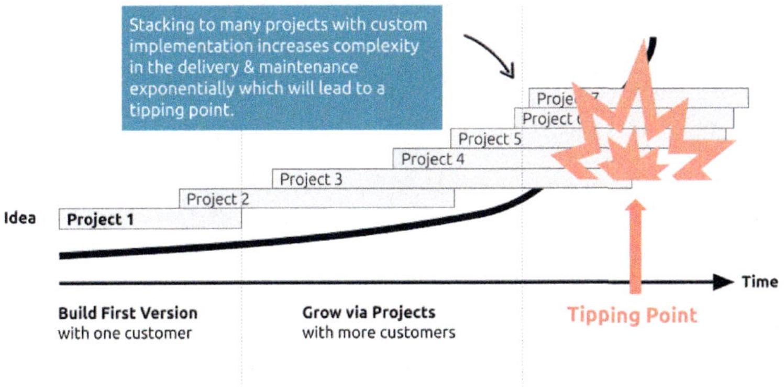

But shifting from project to product mode is not easy. It requires more than new processes, it requires a shift in how the company thinks and collaborates. You need to remodel how the company collectively operates. This book exists to help guide that shift.

Project vs. Product Mode: Key Differences

Understanding the transformation starts with understanding the differences:

Mindset

While project mode organizations focus on the completion of individual, bespoke projects, product mode organizations think in terms of long-term product success. This includes a clear product vision, key performance indicators, and a well-defined target customer or segment.

Sales

In project mode, sales is centred on highly personalized and customized offerings for each customer. Product mode sales, on the other hand, focus on configurable standard solutions that can be tailored through modular add-ons rather than one-off implementations.

Finance

Project mode companies typically operate with a cash flow management mindset, optimizing the use of their employees across billable projects, often bootstrapped. Product mode companies rely more on investment management, making upfront investments in the product with the expectation of returns over time, often supported by debt financing.

Resources and Processes

Project organizations are structured around project managers who oversee resources, timelines, and budgets. Teams are usually assembled for a specific project and disbanded once it is complete. Product organizations rely on product managers who define the roadmap based on a long-term vision and lead durable, cross-functional product teams.

Standardization

In project mode companies, products are often fully customized to meet the specific needs of individual customers. This leads to high variability, duplicated effort, and maintenance overhead. Each implementation becomes a standalone project, diverging from a shared codebase and reducing scalability.

Product companies, in contrast, pursue strategic standardization. They develop a shared core product designed to scale across many customers, while enabling flexibility through structured configuration, themes and plugins, running on a unified platform.

The goal isn't rigid uniformity, it's scalable configurability. Great product organizations focus on enabling variation without compromising code integrity, ensuring speed, maintainability, and customer-specific value.

Code Base

In project mode, each customer or project typically has its own dedicated code base. Product mode companies operate from a single, shared code base used by all customers.

The code base distinction is especially important. Many of the challenges in this book only arise because multiple customers share the same code base, as in most software product businesses.

Hybrid Organizations Are the Norm

In reality, many companies operate somewhere between project and product mode. They may have a standard product, but still deliver large integration projects for key clients. Or they may sell a consulting service while trying to spin out a standalone tool.

Examples of hybrid organizations include:

- Consulting firms launching a product subsidiary
- Corporate spin-offs or joint ventures combining project and product cultures
- Acquired startups trying to stay product-focused within a project-driven parent company
- Internal innovation teams building for internal use, but expected to scale externally

In large enterprises, this hybrid mode is particularly common. Product teams often act as service providers for management and internal stakeholders, which mirrors the customer dynamic of external project companies.

Some companies even run dual models permanently, customizing the product for large clients, while offering a more standard version for smaller ones. We've also seen companies try to move the other way, from product to project. Sometimes, complex customer requirements make this shift unavoidable.

Egg Organizations: A Common Hybrid Structure Explained

In many organizations, product and engineering teams start transitioning into product mode earlier than the rest of the company. They read the latest product books, go to conferences, experiment with discovery, focus on outcomes, and try to shift from feature delivery to problem-solving. But the rest of the organization often still operates in project mode. Oversimplified, the other departments or stakeholders have a feature request, go to engineering and ask for a date when it is ready. Therefore, they treat everything like a small project.

When we first drew the following picture, it looked like an egg in a frying pan, sunny side up. That's why we call it the egg organization: product and engineering think in products, the rest of the company thinks in projects.

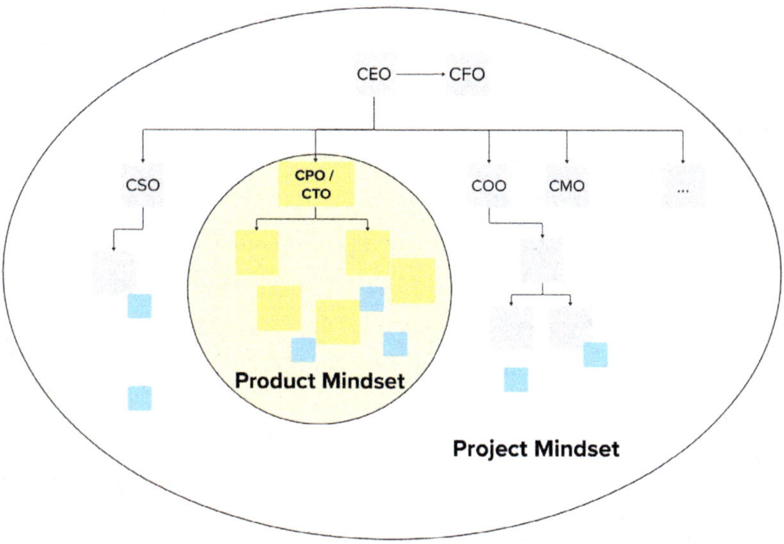

This picture of an egg organisation emerged during a call with a customer, where we mapped his organisation and tried to understand his situation.

The yolk represents the product and engineering teams who want to work in product mode, already trying to work differently. The egg white is the rest of the company, still driven by old expectations and operating models. They hand over feature requests and ask for a shipping date in return.

And no matter how much the yolk intends to move to product mode, it can't break free on its own. The surrounding structure keeps it in project mode.

Is Product Mode Better Than Project Mode?

Not necessarily. It's a strategic decision.

Project businesses can be very successful. Many large consulting firms and software service providers operate this way and generate significant revenue.

Accenture, for example, in 2024 had a global reach with 774,000 people employed and 64 billion euro in sales and 9 billion in free cash flow. The biggest part of their business is based on consulting contracts and therefore a classic project organization.[6] Pretty successful if you ask me. There are also smaller companies. SNP Group, with around 200 million

[6] Accenture Annual Report 2024. https://www.accenture.com/content/dam/accenture/final/accenture-com/a-com-custom-component/iconic/document/Accenture-Fiscal-2024-Annual-Report.pdf. Accessed 25.04.2025.

€ revenue in 2023, has grown by combining consulting and software into a hybrid business.[7]

This book does not argue that product thinking is per se superior. It is a strategic decision. Product businesses are typically more scalable and more profitable. That is the essence of the desire to become a product company. And on the path from a project company towards a product company, you will face a unique set of challenges. That's what this book is about.

Recognizing the Symptoms of Transformation

As companies begin the transformation from project to product, they often experience growing pains. Here are some common symptoms:

- No roadmap that spans all customers
- Sales sells what engineering can't deliver
- Engineers are always in firefighting mode
- Product managers act like backlog translators
- Priorities shift constantly, often based on who shouts the loudest
- Features get promised but not delivered
- Customers receive different versions, creating a "version zoo"
- Estimation processes break down
- Morale drops across teams, often accompanied by fluctuation or burnouts in the leadership team

[7] SNP Group Annual Report: https://investor-relations.snpgroup.com/siteassets/2-publications/archive/de/2023/snp-gb-2023-de.pdf. Accessed 25.04.2025.

These are not causes. They are symptoms. The root causes lie deeper, in structural challenges that affect how the organization works.

In the next chapter, we'll explore the seven core challenges that companies must overcome to complete the transformation.

This is where real product thinking begins.

CHAPTER 2

7 Challenges in the Transformation to a Product Company

Once you've recognized that your company is stuck in project mode, the natural next question is: what's holding us back from transforming into a truly scalable product company? How can we remove the tensions within our organization?

The truth is, transitioning to a product company isn't just about building the right features, it's about changing how your entire organization operates.

As a Product Leader, you're often at the centre of this tension. You're expected to drive product thinking, but you're constantly blocked by old habits, legacy processes, and misaligned incentives across leadership, engineering, and sales.

This chapter is your map of the terrain. We'll walk through the seven most common challenges that companies face when shifting from project to product, and more importantly, how you as a Product Leader can begin to address them.

The 7 challenges are deeply interconnected. If you're struggling with prioritization, chances are you're also dealing with poor product discovery or misaligned pricing. These aren't isolated issues, they're symptoms of a deeper organizational mindset.

To help you understand how project-thinking manifests across your organization, we'll look at seven interconnected areas where product thinking must replace project habits.

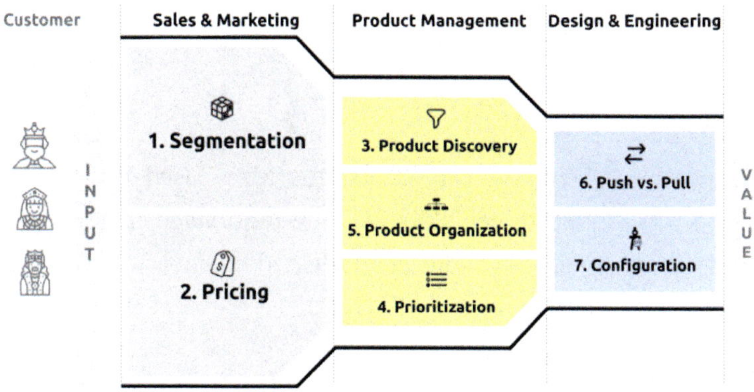

1. Segmentation

In project mode, everything is built around individual customer needs. In product mode, the focus shifts to homogeneous customer segments, groups that share consistent problems and requirements. This shift influences everything from marketing and sales to support and development.

2. Pricing

In a project business, pricing is often based on effort (cost + margin). In a product company, individual customer requests must be priced very high, or rejected altogether, to protect the integrity and scalability of the product. The goal is to serve many customers efficiently, not customized for each one.

3. Product Discovery

In project mode, what gets built is predefined by the customer. No discovery required. In a product mode, product discovery filters ideas based on customer impact and business value. It ensures the team builds what matters, not what was requested.

4. Prioritization

Project companies prioritize based on customer size or urgency and short-term cash. Product companies prioritize based on expected impact across the customer base and long-term value creation. Even after discovery, there are more good ideas than capacity, so a clear prioritization system is critical.

5. Product Organization

Project companies rely on project managers to manage time, scope, and budget. Product companies need empowered product managers and cross-functional teams that optimize for long-term value, not short-term delivery.

6. Push vs. Pull

In project mode, requirements are pushed onto engineering teams. In product mode, teams pull validated opportunities from a shared backlog. This shift improves focus, autonomy, and delivery.

7. Standardization through Configuration

Project mode solutions are built with 100% custom code. Product mode software is designed to enable clients to configure the software themselves and therefore unlock scalability, serving many customers from the same codebase while still allowing flexibility where it matters.

In each of these areas, we'll contrast how project and product companies operate, and show you how to move toward a model that scales.

Our goal in this chapter is to:

✔ Help you diagnose the real barriers to product thinking in your company.
✔ Show how each challenge affects your ability to scale effectively.
✔ Give your language and a mental model to spark the right conversations with leadership and stakeholders.

By the end of this chapter, you'll have a much clearer view of what needs to change, and where you can start.

CHALLENGE 1: Segmentation

Project Sales Seeks Complexity, Product Sales Seeks Standards

Why Segmentation Matters to Product Leaders

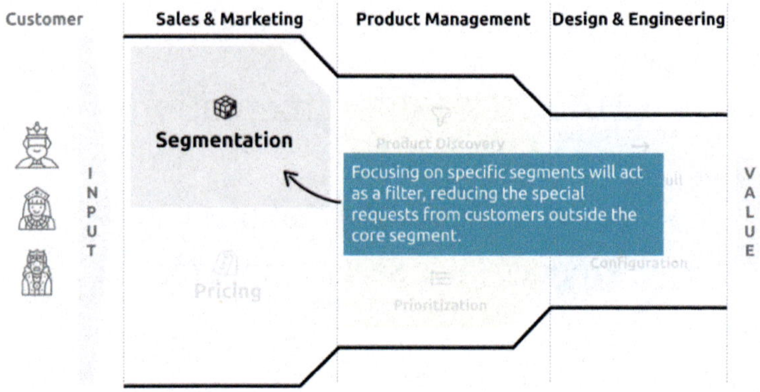

As a Product Leader, you may not own sales, but sales behaviour defines what gets built. If your company still operates with a project mindset, chances are your roadmap is shaped more by deal pressure than product vision. Sales sells the dream; you inherit the delivery.

Understanding how the sales model affects product thinking is key to leading the transition to a scalable product company. This chapter walks you through the mindsets behind project vs. product sales, and how to influence that shift.

The Reality of Project Sales: Complexity Is Good

In project organizations, sales thrive on individual customer demands. Big enterprise deals are celebrated, especially when they involve custom features, long timelines, and complex integrations. Complexity isn't considered a drawback. In fact, it's often viewed as a sales advantage.

The logic typically goes like this:

- Big projects = big revenue = big success.
- Custom requests = more effort = larger deal sizes = success.
- The more tailored a solution feels, the higher its perceived value.

This approach usually starts innocently enough. Imagine a team that builds a new piece of software for a specific customer. It solves the problem perfectly. Soon, the team tries selling it to other customers. The second customer looks at it and says: "*This looks great, but we need a special feature that you currently don't have.*" Since it seems easy enough, the team agrees and builds that unique feature.

Then another customer asks for another unique addition. Maybe it's an extra workflow step, or perhaps integration with a little-known internal system.

At first, these changes seem harmless, just minor tweaks to close important deals. But soon, every new customer comes with a unique set of demands. Before long, your product isn't a single coherent solution. Instead, it's become a Frankenstein product, an assembly of individual parts built for specific customers rather than the market as a whole.

This phenomenon is what we call project stacking: your product grows by continuously adding customer-specific features, not by enhancing your core solution. Over time, your codebase becomes fragile, every new release triggers regressions, and engineering becomes overwhelmed by complexity.

Ultimately, this way of working doesn't lead to long-term success. You're not scaling a product. You're scaling a backlog of promises. The product's complexity becomes unmanageable, customer expectations become impossible to meet, and growth stalls. The solution isn't to add more complexity, it's to shift toward scalable, segment-based product development.

The Mindset of Product Sales: Scale Through Standardization

In product mode, the goal is not to sell complexity, it's to sell standardized value. The product is built once and sold many times. If a feature is added, it should benefit the entire target segment, not just one customer.

The shift in sales behaviour is profound:

- From selling "yes" to selling "this is what we offer."
- From promising everything to qualifying customers who fit the product.
- From closing deals with special features to closing deals with configuration options.

Achieving this demands close alignment between product and sales teams. Sales must have a clear, accurate understanding of the product's capabilities, and its limitations, as well as the rationale behind strategic decisions. Conversely, product teams need to trust salespeople to communicate the roadmap honestly and leverage their direct market exposure to gain more profound insights into customer needs. Sales should be considered strategic partners in product success. Building mutual understanding and respect is key to aligning around shared outcomes.

The 180° Flip in Communication Flow

In a project-driven company, communication flows from the outside in. It's often the customer who defines both the why and the what, with the organization acting as a service provider that builds to order. This might work for bespoke projects or early deals, but it quickly becomes unsustainable at scale.

The Push Model: Customer → Sales → Product → Engineering

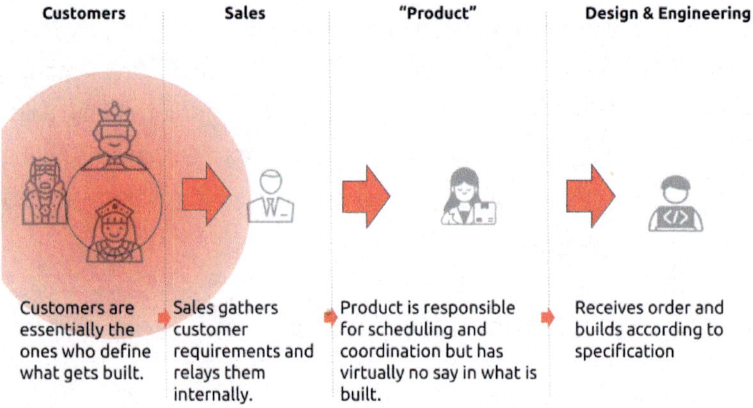

In short: a customer raises a request, sales makes a promise, product tries to accommodate, and engineering is tasked with delivering, often with limited context and tight timelines. It's reactive, fragmented, and difficult to scale. Product doesn't set the direction; it responds to it.

In contrast, a product company flips this flow **from the inside out**:

The Pull Model: Product → Sales & Marketing → Customer Segment

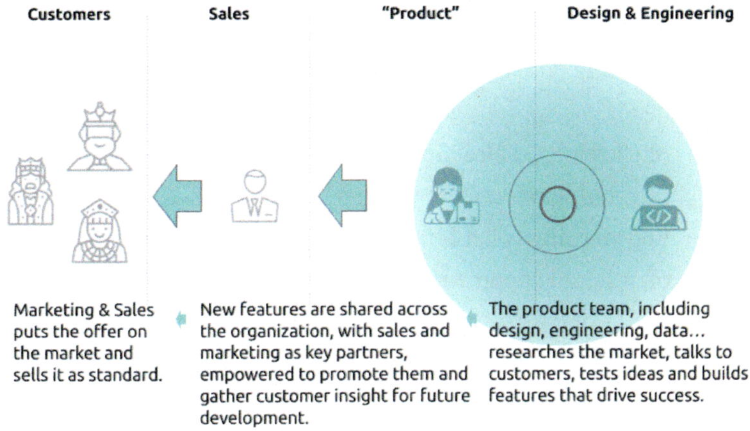

In product mode, responsibility shifts inwards: the organization needs to define why a product exists, what it's supposed to do and who it's supposed to do it for, grounded in validated market needs, not just individual customer requests. This doesn't mean that Product dictates everything. In fact, in most successful companies, Product plays a facilitative role, bringing together input from Sales, Engineering, Design, Leadership, and real users to help the organization focus on the right problems and shape scalable solutions.

Different company cultures split these responsibilities in different ways, but the underlying principle is consistent: someone must frame a compelling "why," and someone must define (and iterate on) the "what." Most often, this means the influence of product increases, while sales evolves from being the voice of individual customers to helping identify and qualify customers who align with the product's direction.

This shift goes beyond improved communication, it's about creating alignment and a sense of shared ownership:

- **Product** facilitates strategy and roadmap development, ensuring both are grounded in real user insights and business needs.
- **Marketing & Sales** aligns its outreach and messaging with the targeted segments the product is built to serve.
- **Engineering** collaborates to deliver high-impact work based on validated opportunities, not unvetted feature requests.

For this to work, Product must bring not just ideas, but also clarity and evidence, making it easier for other teams to trust in the product direction. Sales will only defer to product-led guidance if they believe the roadmap is credible, tied to measurable outcomes, and their incentive scheme supports the new model.

This organizational shift also calls for new rituals that foster collaboration and transparency:

- Regular product updates that give the company visibility into what's launching, why it matters, and how to position it.
- Shared enablement tools, like segment-specific sales decks tied to roadmap goals.
- A strong, structured intake process for feedback, coupled with transparency around what gets prioritized and why.

When done well, this shift transforms Product from a reactive service function into a strategic facilitator, one that empowers teams to work together toward a clear, customer-centred, and scalable product vision.

What You Can Do as a Product Leader

✔Start with segmentation

Collaborating with sales to assess the current customer base is typically our first step. A simple yet impactful approach is to initially divide existing customers into two groups: those using standard products and those with custom code adjustments. See the best practice example which follows.

✔Enable marketing & sales to sell the product you actually have. Develop sales materials that highlight the product's strengths, roadmap, and strategic direction. Show them how to sell what exists.

✔Align sales incentives

Sales needs to be incentivized in an aligned way to the product model. If the incentives are targeted towards projects, it is in everybody's interest to calibrate. It is not within your responsibility as product leader to change it, but you can start the discussion and make the impact transparent.

✔Participate in sales conversations

Join key deals early to guide expectations and qualify fit. This helps shift the perception of product from "gatekeeper" to "strategic partner."

Best Practice: Segmenting by Customization Effort

One company we coached mapped their past deals by how much engineering effort each one required. They defined three buckets:

1. **High effort** – Full custom-builds. Project mode. High revenue, lower margins.
2. **Medium effort** – Tailoring existing features.
3. **Low effort** – Standard product. Lower revenue, higher margin.

The surprising insight? The best-fit customers came from medium-sized businesses in one vertical, who required only light configuration. They weren't the biggest names, yielded lower total revenue numbers, but they were profitable, fast to onboard, and compatible with a product-first approach.

This triggered a strategic pivot. The company refocused its sales team on this segment, introduced tighter qualification criteria, increased price for custom features. Eventually, they stopped an offer in the process which would have yielded several million euros to focus on the medium-sized companies. Going forward, they would only accept big and complex deals that would align with the strategic long-term vision. A great advancement in the focus of the organization and the ability to say no to things which are not aligned with the long-term vision.

The result: faster delivery, lower revenue per customer was offset by the total number of customers. Therefore, profitability increased, happier engineers and a better product.

Best Practice: Fixing Sales Incentives to Match Product Thinking

One blocker in transitioning from project to product sales isn't mindset, it's money. In many companies, sales reps are rewarded for closing big deals, regardless of complexity or alignment with the product roadmap.

The larger and more custom the deal, the higher the commission and addition to sales quota.

This creates a dangerous misalignment: sales behaviour optimizes for revenue, while product and engineering pay the price in complexity and delivery risk.

As a Product Leader, you likely don't own the compensation model. That is why you must highlight its impact on the whole organization. Gather data (share of maintenance work, features built for single customer etc.) to illustrate the downside of serving individual customers. And then you need to partner with sales and finance leadership to explore changes such as:

- Higher commission on standardized deals within the core product offering.
- Lower or no commission for custom development work.
- Incentives for land-and-expand strategies over large custom deals.
- Recognition programs for segment-fit deals that lead to lower churn and faster onboarding.

Realigning incentives will ultimately benefit all participants. Sales and Marketing might have to adapt, but will benefit from scalability and easier delivery in the long run. Without it, even the best product strategy will be undermined by how deals are closed.

Why This Challenge Sets the Tone for All Others

Sales behaviour directly impacts:

- **Pricing** – If you sell custom work at product prices, you're underfunding engineering (Challenge 2).
- **Discovery & Prioritization** – If every deal is unique, you'll never validate at scale (Challenges 3 & 4).
- **Engineering Load** – If sales keeps saying yes, your teams are permanently overcommitted (Challenge 6).
- **Configurability** – If the roadmap is random, there's no time to build a real configurable platform (Challenge 7).

If your company wants to become a scalable product company, sales must evolve too. And as a Product Leader, you can either fight every deal, or help change how deals are shaped in the first place.

Test Your Own Company

Test your company with the **Project to Product Self-Assessment** by scanning the code or go to: product-masterclass.com/p2passessment

CHALLENGE 2: Pricing

Stop Undervaluing Custom Work

Why Pricing Matters to Product Leaders

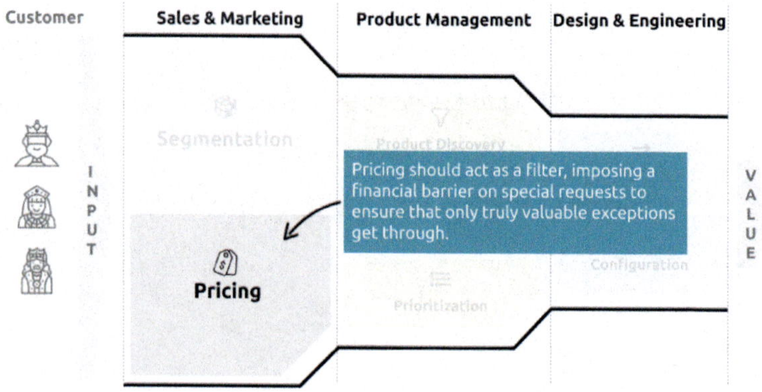

There are fundamental differences between how pricing works in project mode versus product mode.

In project mode, custom features are usually priced using a basic formula: cost plus margin. But this model systematically underestimates the real complexity involved. It rarely accounts for the full engineering effort, especially the long-term operational and maintenance costs. As a result, custom features are often priced too low or bundled into deals for free just to close a contract, which ultimately will lead to an underfunded engineering with too little resources.

In product mode, pricing must reflect value, not effort. That value might be tied to usage volume, core functionality, or measurable business outcomes. The goal is to design pricing structures that reward scale, encourage standardization, and support long-term sustainability, not one-off exceptions.

Special features for single customers should be priced unintuitively high, intentionally so. This isn't about maximizing margin; it's about sending a clear signal. High pricing acts as a built-in complexity tax and compensates for the hidden long-term costs: increased code complexity, additional QA effort, ongoing support, and slower product evolution. Used correctly, pricing becomes a strategic lever.

Product and engineering might not set the price, but they absolutely live with the consequences. Underpriced custom work creates bloated backlogs, tech debt, and a constant drain on your team's capacity. It confuses priorities and dilutes focus.

That's why aligning pricing logic with product thinking isn't optional, it's essential. It protects your team's time, your roadmap's clarity, and your product's long-term health.

How Project Companies Price

In project mode, pricing is primarily effort-based:

The company estimates the engineering effort and adds a margin, say, 25%, or 30%, to set the sales price.

The issue? These estimates are routinely optimistic, charging far too little, with the result that the company cannot afford to hire more software engineers to increase needed capacity accordingly. The “overoptimistic charging” is due to various factors. Here is an incomplete short list of the most important factors:

1. **Anchored in Delivery, Not Lifecycle**
   Project pricing usually stops at “what does it take to ship this feature?” But the real cost includes everything that happens after shipping: edge cases, bugs, compatibility maintenance, upgrades, migrations, internal enablement, etc. These costs are invisible at the quote stage, but they hit hard later.

2. **Engineering Is Pressured to Say “Yes”**
   In the sales process, you often need fast estimates to close deals. Engineering is either not involved early or gives ballpark numbers under time pressure. No one wants to be the blocker or lose the deal, so the estimate gets shaved down to “what's possible if everything goes right,” which it never does.

3. **The Hidden Cost of Variation**
   One-off features frequently introduce entirely new behaviours, edge cases, or integrations. These increase regression risk exponentially. But because this complexity isn't obvious upfront, and isn't tracked, it doesn't get priced in.

And it even gets worse, if the sales team closes a deal and throws in minor custom features "free of charge" to win the contract or these features are built for a single customer and provide no additional value to the broader market.

Overall, this creates a false sense of profitability. The feature may appear to have low delivery cost on paper, but the long-term cost is high. Not only financially, but also in terms of engineering capacity.

Imagine the maintenance work after a feature is shipped, is like a small stone in a hiker's backpack. On its own, it seems insignificant. But collect enough of them, and suddenly, your backpack is half full, leaving little room for anything new. Every tiny exception adds weight, and over time, it's not the big features that slow you down. It's the accumulation of small, "quick" fixes, the amount of small stones that become heavy, quietly drain your capacity, and limit your ability to move forward.[8]

How Product Companies Price

When companies move from project mode to product mode, pricing shifts from tracking effort to capturing value at scale. In project work, it's possible to assign a price based on hours worked. But in product companies, you're building once and selling many times, sometimes to hundreds, thousands, or millions of users.

That changes everything. You can't trace effort to a specific customer any more. Instead, product pricing is shaped by one central question:

How much value does this product (or feature) create for our customer segment, and how much of that value can we claim? [9]

---

[8] This analogy was brought to us by Uwe Kunath and we love and use this analogy since then: https://www.linkedin.com/in/uwe-kunath-a8770595/

[9] From Zero to One: Notes on Startups, or How to Build the Future by Peter Thiel, Blake Masters.

Most product companies rely on two primary pricing dimensions: volume and functionality.

1. Volume-Based Pricing

Volume-based pricing links the price to how much the product is used. This includes units like:

- Users per month
- API calls per day
- Transactions processed
- Seats or licences
- Data stored or bandwidth used

The logic: as the customer's usage grows, so does the value they receive, and your revenue grows with it. Here are some examples:

Mailchimp charges based on the number of emails sent. The more a customer uses the tool, the more value it provides, and the more they pay.

Stripe takes a cut from each transaction processed. If your customers make more money, so does Stripe.

2. Feature-Based Pricing

In feature-based pricing, customers pay based on what functionality is unlocked. This often shows up as:

- Tiered packages (e.g. Basic, Pro, Enterprise)
- Add-on modules for specific use cases

- All-in-one bundles that grow in value with each feature layer

The logic: more functionality = more value = higher price.

Here are also some examples:

Microsoft 365 offers multiple pricing tiers. Higher tiers include more tools: Word, Excel, SharePoint, Teams, etc. Each tier gives more utility to the customer.

HubSpot sells multiple integrated modules: CRM, Marketing, Sales, Service. Customers can buy a single module, but if they add more, the combined value increases significantly.

These two dimensions are typically the most important pricing measurements. Of course, they can also be combined to create more complex models. This will be easy for you to spot in the wild.

Product-Led Growth: Pricing One Dimension at Zero

To enable product-led growth, many SaaS companies strategically price one of these two dimensions, volume or functionality, at zero cost. This lowers the barrier to entry, encourages user adoption, and lets customers experience core value before committing to a paid plan.

Mailchimp offers a "Forever Free" plan that includes up to 6,000 emails per month, giving users real utility before they hit a paywall.[10]

---

[10] Mailchimp Pricing Overview: https://mailchimp.com/de/pricing/marketing/compare-plans/?currency=EUR. Accessed 25.04.2025.

Canva follows a similar logic: the basic version includes generous functionality, while premium features like advanced design tools, premium templates, and a vast stock-image library are locked behind a paywall.[11]

This approach turns the product into the primary acquisition channel, reducing the need for heavy sales upfront and allowing the pricing model to scale with customer success.

How Product Companies Price Special Requests

Custom feature requests are a different beast. While volume and functionality pricing are designed for scale, custom work threatens it. A feature built for one customer adds long-term complexity for testing, maintenance, documentation, and onboarding. These costs are real, even if they're invisible at the start.

That's why product companies must price custom features intentionally high, not just to recoup costs, but to impose a deliberate complexity tax. It forces the organization to pause and ask: Is this exception worth it? Is it aligned with our product vision?

If the answer is no, the right move is to decline the request or even better, set a price which will overcompensate for the effort and make the customer decline.

To give you an emphasis, how that can look like, overcompensating could mean charging 5x the engineering effort. The bigger companies

[11] Canva Pricing Overview: https://www.canva.com/en/pricing/. Accessed 25.04.2025.

get, these deliberate complexity taxes will get higher. We even heard of companies charging 50x the effort, just to ensure the standard software keeps being a standard.

Pricing Mindset: From Controlling to Investor

In project mode, pricing is often leveraged primarily to secure deals. The core questions become centred around how much to charge and how quickly deals can be closed, and if they are profitable at the "end of the project". This creates a risky illusion, because one-off revenue alone doesn't clarify whether a feature, customer, or deal truly contributes long-term value.

Revenue is simply what you earn, while Return on Investment (ROI) tells you whether it's genuinely worth it.

Transitioning to a product-mindset means shifting from controlling costs to strategically investing resources. Rather than asking about immediate costs to build, the focus shifts toward understanding the long-term value created for both customers and the company.

This strategic shift impacts every pricing decision, prompting deeper considerations about whether features will drive sustainable growth or create unnecessary complexity, the true ongoing costs of maintaining and supporting features, and alignment with target segments, broader strategies, and product visions.

This isn't about cutting costs, it's about sharpening your focus. Each feature developed is essentially a strategic bet. Successful companies manage these bets thoughtfully, emphasizing metrics like ROI, cost of delay, and strategic alignment rather than simply focusing on short-term revenue per deal. In product mode, the objective becomes investing in scalable, cumulative value.

Watch the interview with Jeff Bezos[12]

Jeff Bezos, the founder of Amazon, provides a clear example of this mindset. He said in an interview that Amazon is based on 3 pillars that never change: 1. fast delivery, 2. vast selection, and 3. low prices. Bezos observed that no customer would ever ask for slower shipping, fewer choices, or higher prices, highlighting that small improvements in these areas would compound significantly over time. Amazon continuously invests in enhancements that might appear minor yet align precisely with their long-term strategy. Adopting an investor mindset requires discipline to optimize for long-term success, clarity to avoid distractions, and courage to strategically invest, recognizing the significant potential of incremental improvements over time. Consider carefully what your company is optimizing for, whether it be revenue, growth, profitability, or strategic alignment. There's no incorrect answer, but having a clear, intentional focus is essential.

Ultimately, your pricing strategy reflects your mindset, and your mindset shapes your product, roadmap, and organizational future.

What You Can Do as a Product Leader

✔Assess your company's "complexity tax rate"

Sit down and estimate your "tax rate". You can do that by estimating your share of maintenance in the engineering department. Complexity Tax Rate = Capacity Required for Maintenance / Total Engineering Capacity. A rough estimation will be sufficient. Make that share transparent to other leaders, and discuss the concepts shown above to add the complexity tax to future offerings.

✔Design modular pricing structures

If you do not have it yet, create pricing models that allow for scalable variability, e.g., usage-based pricing, feature bundles, configuration tiers.

✔Say no with confidence

If a feature doesn't serve your broader customer base and isn't priced accordingly, it's okay to decline. The thing is, you are not the one calling the shots. Amazon has 3 dimensions they optimize for, which will be true in 10 years from now. What are your companies 3 dimensions?

Best Practice: Pricing as a Strategic Filter

One company we advised had long struggled with a familiar problem: sales routinely offered custom features to close deals, and the product was left holding the bag. The backlog was overflowing, engineering was buried in one-off requests, and the product vision had become a wishlist of unrelated features.

To change this, the leadership team introduced a two-track pricing model:

- **Track 1:** Standard product features and capabilities, bundled into predictable pricing tiers across customer segments. These were built once and sold repeatedly.

- **Track 2:** Custom requests from enterprise clients, which were routed through a cross-functional pricing and product steering committee. Each request was assessed not just for revenue potential, but for alignment with product strategy and delivery capacity. If approved, the work was priced at a significant premium and capacity explicitly blocked in the teams and visible on the roadmap...

This model didn't just bring structure, it shifted mindsets:

- Sales began to question the value of custom promises before making them.
- Custom requests were no longer cheap giveaways, they came with visible costs, both in pricing and roadmap tradeoffs.
- Product leaders were able to protect roadmap clarity and delivery velocity, knowing which work had been explicitly accepted and properly resourced.

If necessary, you can even go one step further and tie sales commission or quota to deal types. Full commission is paid on standard deals that match the core product strategy. For heavily customized deals, commissions are reduced, not paid at all, or even deducting other commissions, reflecting the additional overhead and risk those deals introduce.

The result? Sales behaviour will change dramatically. Reps become more thoughtful about fit, start pushing standard offerings more consistently, and help drive customer expectations toward what the product can sustainably support.

These approaches do not just improve pricing, it puts product back in the driver's seat.

Why This Challenge Undermines Product Focus

Undervalued custom work is a silent killer of velocity & product strategy. If complexity is cheap, your roadmap becomes crowded with exceptions. Your team loses speed, clarity, and motivation.

Pricing may feel like someone else's job, but the downstream impact lands on product & engineering. If you want to build a value-focused product org, your company needs a value-focused pricing logic.

Test Your Own Company

Test your company with the **Project to Product Self-Assessment** by scanning the code or go to: product-masterclass.com/p2passessment

CHALLENGE 3: Product Discovery

Projects Don't Need Discovery.
Products Need It to Filter.

Why Product Discovery Matters to Product Leaders

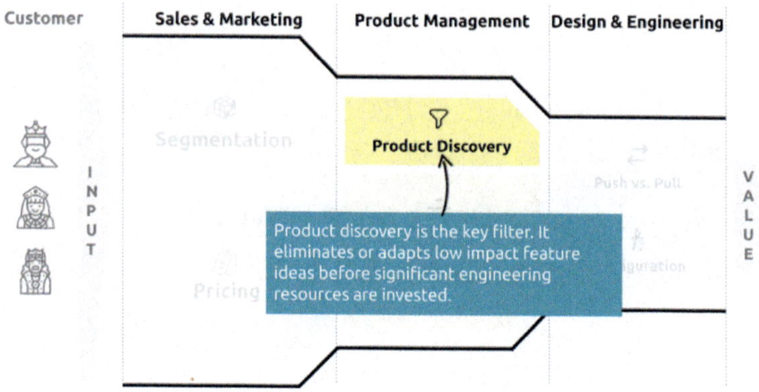

One of the core differences between project and product companies lies in how they decide what to build[12]. In a project company, the customer defines the scope, and the team delivers exactly what was ordered. There is no need to ask why because the "what" is already set. In a product company, the goal isn't to deliver a predefined scope, but to identify and solve the most valuable problems for a broader set of customers, thus maximizing long-term value for customers and growth for your company alike.

And yet, many companies trying to move from project to product mode fail to build this muscle. Instead of thoughtful filtering, they treat all incoming requests the same. Feature requests from customers, sales, or stakeholders are added to the backlog without clear evaluation. In short,

---

[12]https://www.svpg.com/books/transformed-moving-to-the-product-operating-model/

there is no product discovery, only a growing list of demands and expectations.

This is where your role as a Product Leader becomes critical. You cannot build everything, and you shouldn't. And you need to make that clear.

There are always more ideas in a company than people who can implement them. Always. This is the situation, where product managers come into play to find out what to do. Product management means saying no, no to ideas that lack evidence, no to features that don't align with the strategy, and no to requests that won't deliver value at scale.

How Project Companies Handle Discovery (or Don't)

In project companies, product discovery is often nonexistent or reduced to a few clarifying conversations. The customer defines the feature; your job is to deliver it. There is no reason to question the request or dig deeper.

But that same approach breaks down when applied to product development:

- Teams take every request at face value.
- Every suggestion is treated as urgent and valid.
- Delivery becomes a race to build, not a process to think.

In this context, product teams frequently feel like they're working in a feature factory, just building what stakeholders or clients want. But the goal of a product company is to build a value factory, where each feature contributes to meaningful customer outcomes or tackles an additional customer segment.

How Product Companies Use Discovery to Filter

In a true product company, discovery is a core discipline. It's how product teams ensure they build what matters, not just what's requested. Instead of jumping straight from idea to backlog, they:

- Explore the underlying problem behind the feature request.
- Ask who else experiences this issue and how frequently.
- Check if it aligns with the company's product strategy and customer segments.
- Run lightweight validation: interviews, prototypes, shadowing, or usage analytics.
- Test if clients are willing to commit to solutions and pay

Discovery is not about slowing down, it's about building confidence before building things. When done well, it:

- Filters out noise before it reaches engineering.
- Aligns teams on what success looks like.
- Prevents waste and builds momentum through smaller iterations.

Validated ideas move forward. Everything else is documented, discussed, and, if needed, politely declined or offered with an overcompensating price.

Definition: What Does a Product Manager Actually Do?

In project companies, "product managers" are often reduced to ticket managers or delivery coordinators doing project work. But in a product company, the role is very different:

A Product Manager is not responsible for executing what others request. A Product Manager is responsible for finding the most valuable problems to solve and ensuring the team builds the right solutions to deliver value.

That means they:

- Talk to customers regularly.
- Understand the market context.
- Translate vague input into clear problem statements.
- Push back when ideas don't make sense.
- Prioritize based on impact, not volume.

In short, they are not backlog managers. They are strategic filters.

The Organizational Reality

Many product teams already know how discovery works, at least in theory. They've read the books. They've been to the conferences. Furthermore, they fully comprehend it.

So why isn't it happening?

Because the rest of the organization isn't ready and perceives it as additional work.

In most hybrid organizations, sales still sell timelines. Delivery or implementation teams are responsible for execution. Customer Success is tasked with driving adoption and managing client expectations. Leadership craves certainty. CFOs prioritize predictability in revenue and cost. Almost everyone outside of product and engineering still sees the world through a project lens: scope defined upfront, success measured by shipping on time and within budget. Stakeholders typically know exactly what they want and think, that it is certain, that the solution will work. Therefore, from their perspective, no further discovery or validation is needed.

In that world, discovery is not encouraged. It is not needed. It's considered a delay. The roadmap is already full, and the company expects delivery, not questions.

This is the real challenge. Discovery isn't just a product technique, it's an **organizational mindset shift**. And as a Product Leader, you need to champion that shift, even when you don't have direct authority to make it happen.

Best Practice: How to Drag Your Organization into Discovery

Let's face it: project-driven organizations typically resist discovery because they associate it with delays, uncertainty, or simply don't see the value because they already "know" what needs to get built. Here's How You Can Turn This Situation Around for Yourself

Many features fail, that's a fact. But stakeholders often believe they are "certain" making discovery feel like an unnecessary delay. Use this knowledge to your advantage to gradually build negotiation leverage over time. This is actually simple to execute: Before implementing a feature, thoroughly discuss and define its expected outcome together with stakeholders. Clearly differentiate and define success at multiple levels: output, outcome, and impact, along with measurable criteria for each.

Output vs. Outcome vs. Impact[14]

Once implemented, you win regardless of the outcome

- **If successful**, great! You've delivered tangible value.
- **If unsuccessful**, use this as leverage during future requests by posing a simple yet powerful question: "What makes us sure that this feature will succeed this time?"

This question inherently advocates for product discovery, aligning your interests with those of the stakeholders. As a product professional, proactively support stakeholders by suggesting practical ways to break down the new feature, conduct quick prototype testing, and engage engineers and designers early to validate customer behaviour in a timely manner.

Once you've successfully guided stakeholders through this experience, you'll have built enough trust to advocate for integrating this iterative and evidence-based approach into the organization's standard processes.

Defining success metrics upfront and measuring outcomes becomes your Trojan horse for introducing and institutionalizing product discovery.

What You Can Do as a Product Leader

✓Start where you are
Even if you can't implement full discovery just yet, begin by talking to customers, gathering data and smaller tests. This is just the extra mile, every PM and product leader needs to go and will equip you with arguments in discussions about what to build.

✓Discover high stake features
Teams often make the mistake of discovering things that are not significant, button colour, small features, you name it. Start with the opposite: take the biggest initiative, epic, or feature in your backlog. This will ensure your work is relevant. Discovery is risk management, so start with the biggest risk, which is most likely the biggest feature.

✓Drag stakeholders into discovery
The reality is: most features fail. Use that to your advantage. Make sure you write down the expectations for each feature before developing it. If it fails, you will have negotiation leverage next time asking: "What makes us so sure, this feature will be a success? How can we invest to test?" This way you drag stakeholders into discovery.

✓Break features down to smaller versions for stakeholders
No stakeholder wants to invest in discovery because it takes time. Just rephrase it. Ship the first stripped down version fast but ensure to

include usage or impact measurement. Sounds logical for the stakeholder and is essentially discovery.

Why This Challenge Is a Turning Point

Without discovery, product teams are just feature delivery teams. They're stuck executing decisions made elsewhere. With discovery, they become strategic drivers.

Discovery is how you build alignment, earn trust, and shift the organization from project delivery to product thinking.

This is where real product management begins.

Test Your Own Company

Test your company with the **Project to Product Self-Assessment** by scanning the code or go to: product-masterclass.com/p2passessment

CHALLENGE 4: Prioritization

When Everything Is Important, Nothing Gets Done

Why Prioritization Matters to Product Leaders

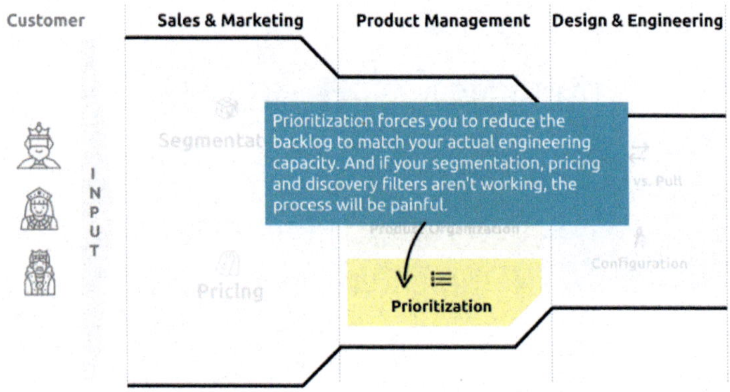

Prioritization is not just about choosing what to do next, it's about focus and alignment. In successful product companies, prioritization helps teams channel their limited resources toward the highest-impact opportunities. But in hybrid companies stuck between project and product thinking, prioritization becomes political, reactive, and chaotic.

Every department has its list. Every stakeholder has their must-haves. And without strong product leadership and a shared strategy for evaluating what matters most, the backlog becomes a battlefield.

As a Product Leader, you're not just managing priorities, you're managing expectations, tensions, and trade-offs. Your job is to protect your team from becoming a dumping ground for everyone else's urgency.

How Project Companies Prioritize

In project-driven companies, prioritization is usually based on contract value, customer size, or executive influence. The logic is simple:

- Big customers get what they want.
- Internal stakeholders lobby for their initiatives.
- Salespeople escalate deal blockers.

If you want to summarize it in a short, illustrative formula, it would be:

Importance of the customer

X perceived urgency (e.g. expressed by noise or escalations)

X existing contractual penalties (or other unpleasant consequences)

= Prioritization of the feature

There's rarely a mechanism to weigh ideas based on value and impact, feasibility, or strategic fit. Instead, the team just builds what's most urgent, or loudest.

This works when delivering one-off projects, but it collapses in product development. With multiple customer segments, shared infrastructure, and limited capacity, prioritization must be more than gut feeling.

The Root Cause of Dysfunctional Prioritization

Ironically, the root cause often isn't the prioritization method itself. There are plenty of books and literature about the different prioritization frameworks. We would rather not repeat them here.

Because the reason they fail to deliver results is somewhere else: It's the lack of upstream filtering. It is not the method you use to prioritize that makes the difference, it is the process and structure in your company that makes or breaks things. Let's go through the steps, why prioritization is dysfunctional in many companies:

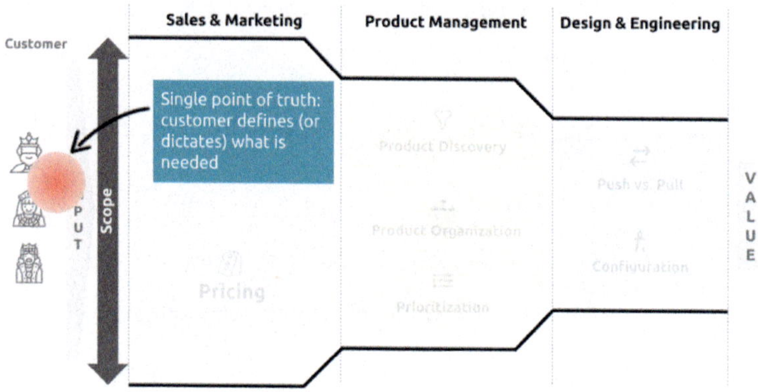

It all starts with collecting feature requests from customers. A few large and therefore important clients articulate what they want. Your CEO, CSO, or Customer Success Management collects these requests, sometimes even adds more features as discussed in challenge 1 & 2 and pushes the features into the organization. How could building exactly what the customer wants possibly be wrong? Here is the catch: But rather than simplifying the system, this behaviour injects complexity into every step that follows, spreading it downstream into prioritization, delivery, testing, and maintenance.

By the way, this is one of the main differences between B2B and B2C. In B2C you typically do not have a couple of strong customer voices, but many smaller voices and segments with different demands. Having many directions to go puts the company in a different position: you need to decide early on, who you serve, and what is the core of the company. Having this clarity early on, will make B2C companies naturally avoid many of the challenges presented in this book

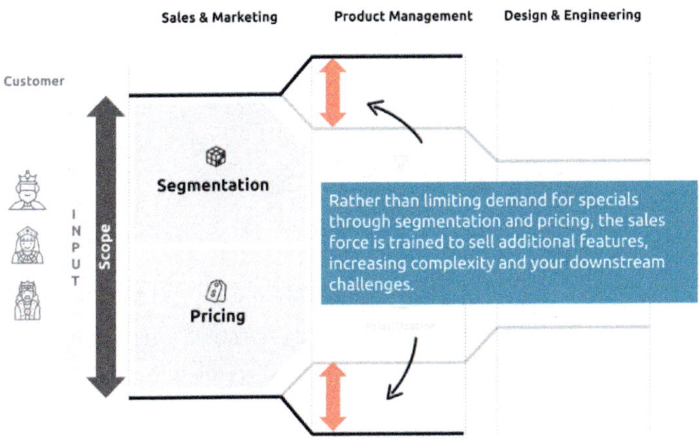

When no segmentation is in place, too many special feature requests get through. If pricing is not used as a strategic tool to filter unimportant wishes, then, your strategy isn't clear, every idea seems equally valid. Both filters dysfunctional will lead to a high variety of special requests landing on the "product managers" table.

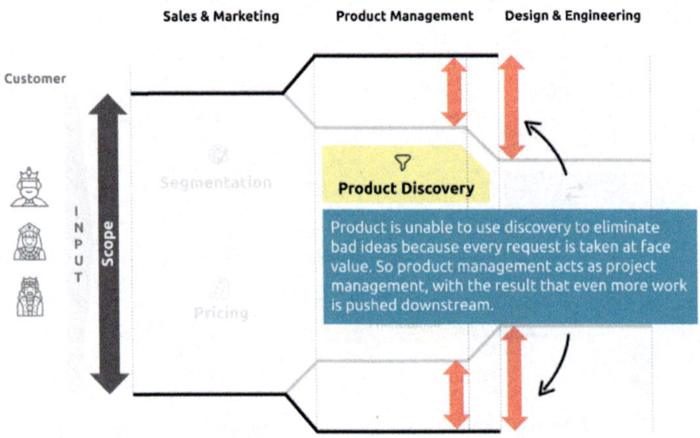

Product managers are not empowered to do their job and see if the suggested features and functions will generate value across many customers. There was already a commitment to the clients earlier in the process, giving product managers little room for adaptation. They are trapped between the requests and the timelines to deliver, essentially acting as a project manager.

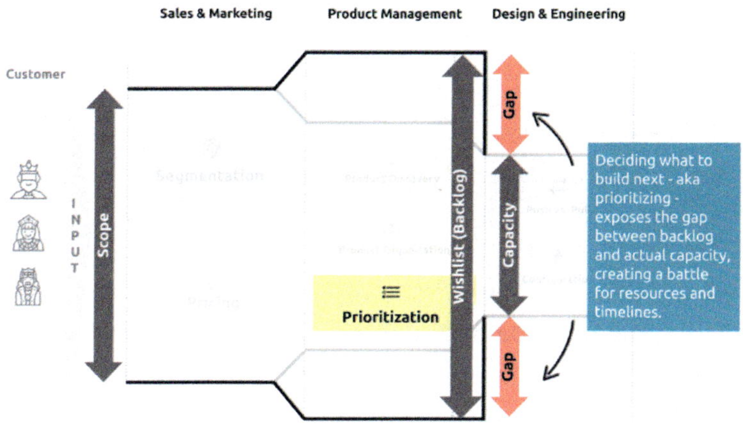

At the end of the funnel, the crux will become obvious: too many things in the backlog, too little capacity to build. And so, prioritization becomes the place where all the company's dysfunction shows up.

In a project company, prioritization is a task of resource allocation and workload balancing to ensure timely delivery. We are dealing with conflicts and escalations, we are firefighting to meet immediate customer or contractual requirements.

Project mode prioritization is about efficient delivery on predefined commitments. It is about "what needs to be done first" (urgency) rather than "what matters most strategically" (importance)

What Changes in Product Companies

Here is the thing: as a project company, you never need to say NO. The wildest feature request? No problem, challenge accepted: here is our estimate, if the customer is willing to pay, let's go!

In product companies, this is not possible any more. You need to start saying NO to something at some point. You have to define a border of what you want to do and what not. This border is typically called strategy. In that sense, strategy is telling you what you will NOT do as much as it tells you what you intend to do.

Prioritization reflects strategy. It ensures that what teams choose to do (and not do) moves the company toward its defined goals.

It's not merely selecting tasks or ranking features; it's about:

- Directing limited resources (time, money, talent) toward activities that maximize long-term business impact.
- Clarifying strategic choices by explicitly deciding what the company will and will not do.
- Reducing organizational complexity by setting clear boundaries, thus avoiding continuous debates and decision fatigue.
- Synchronizing different departments and stakeholders, creating shared understanding about what truly matters.
- Enabling agility and adaptability, ensuring the company can swiftly redirect efforts to emerging opportunities or threats.

Ultimately, prioritization is the tangible decision that translates business strategy into action, becoming the critical link between strategy and operational execution.

Practical Suggestion: Prioritizing Without Clear Strategic Guardrails

When shifting from project mode to product mode, product leaders often find themselves lacking strategic direction. Without these guardrails, prioritization quickly becomes difficult or politically charged. Since many companies transitioning from project mode typically don't have an explicit product strategy in place yet, you as a product leader must bridge this gap temporarily.

A practical solution is to define your own lightweight, provisional strategy. Start by identifying who your main customers really are (see challenge 1), and what critical problems they share and which dimensions will keep stable over time (remember the Amazon case above). Then set clear, short-term, measurable objectives, such as improving customer retention or increasing onboarding success.

Communicate this provisional "mini-strategy" transparently within your organization. Make clear to stakeholders that although it's not yet the full-fledged product strategy, it provides a necessary and immediate basis for making decisions. This approach replaces urgency-based, politically driven prioritization with measurable and customer-focused prioritization.

Use your prioritization decisions as opportunities to test and validate your assumptions about customer needs and business impact. Run small experiments that yield quick results, then transparently share these insights across your organization. This builds trust and credibility in your approach.

Over time, as you gather evidence of successful prioritization decisions, leverage these wins to advocate for broader strategic conversations. Highlight concrete outcomes to senior management, demonstrating the tangible benefits of strategic clarity. Gradually involve stakeholders across departments in refining and formalizing the provisional strategy, slowly evolving it into clear and actionable strategic guardrails.

This approach allows you to immediately establish effective prioritization practices, even without existing strategic guidance, while organically cultivating the long-term strategic clarity your organization needs.

What You Can Do as a Product Leader

✔**Create your own mini product strategy** – If there is a lack of strategy and guidance, clarify your own picture: what is our core segment the company should chase? What do these customers need? Can we measure the hypothesis?

✔**Create a transparent prioritization model** – Make your decision criteria visible and explain them. Start somewhere and collect data to iterate your strategy. You should also do that if decisions are against your opinion of what to do next. Measure success metrics and let the customer decide.

✔**Push back to noise** – Saying no is part of the job. Say it with data, not ego.

✔**Make discovery work** – Don't let unvalidated ideas compete with high-impact opportunities. Therefore, use the strategies presented in the product discovery section to improve things in the long run.

Why Prioritization Reveals the Impact of Earlier Challenges

Prioritization problems are often symptoms, not root causes. If you're struggling to say no, it may be because:

- You didn't validate ideas (Challenge 3).
- You don't know what creates value (Challenge 2).
- You're building for everyone or individual customers (Challenge 1).

Fix those, and prioritization gets easier. Leave them untouched, and even the best prioritization framework will feel like chaos.

Test Your Own Company

Test your company with the **Project to Product Self-Assessment** by scanning the code or go to: product-masterclass.com/p2passessment

CHALLENGE 5: Product Organization

Great Products Don't Come From Project Structures.

Why It Matters How You Structure Your Product Organization

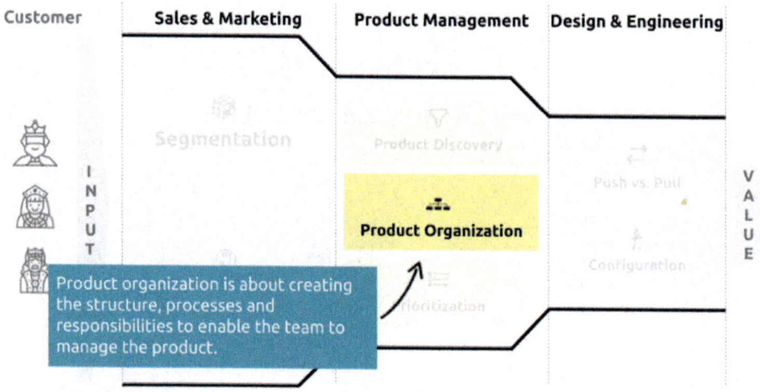

You can't deliver great products in an organization built to deliver projects. That's the core of this challenge. Most companies are structured for predictability, timelines, and stakeholder management, not for learning, iteration, and customer outcomes. To truly operate in product mode, you must rethink three key building blocks: your org structure, your roles, and responsibilities, and how well your teams are enabled to make smart product decisions.

1. Org Structure: From Delivery Machines to Outcome Owners

Going from client-based teams to solution- or value-focused teams may sound like a basic move to experienced product professionals. And yes, you're right. But the reality is that many organizations are still stuck in structures built around their first client, a key enterprise contract, or years of reselling heavily customized software. These setups don't exist because people don't know better. They're the result of organic growth and a history of trying to survive, win business, and deliver.

Changing this structure is the first real step toward product mode. It creates the conditions for everything else, product strategy, discovery, and empowered teams, to actually work. Without structural change, even the best intentions fall apart under the weight of legacy systems and stakeholder-driven chaos.

Books like *Empowered* and *Inspired* by Marty Cagan lay out clear guidance for high-performing product organizations. They describe practices such as empowered product trios, outcome-driven roadmaps, continuous discovery, and solving of real user problems, not just building what's been requested. But all of these practices require the basics to be right. And that starts with how teams are structured.

In many project mode organizations, teams are typically structured as mere delivery units. They reflect major clients, internal departments, or technologies. This leads to fragmented ownership, excessive handoffs, and constant coordination overhead. Product managers are stretched thin across multiple teams, often reduced to being go-betweens for stakeholders and delivery teams. No one owns the full user journey or problem space end-to-end. Teams are reactive, waiting for prioritized backlogs or delivery briefs rather than driving outcomes.

Product mode flips this model. Teams are designed around customer problems, journeys, or business outcomes, not legacy systems or siloed functions. These teams are durable (they stay with a problem space over time), cross-functional (including product, design, engineering, and often data), and mission-driven (focused on delivering continuous impact, not just completing projects).

Each team should have a clearly defined scope of ownership. That could be a part of the user journey (e.g., onboarding for new customers), a product metric (e.g., increasing activation), or a business-critical flow (e.g., checkout or upsell). The goal is clarity on who owns what, and what success looks like.

This structural shift doesn't just improve accountability. It accelerates learning. When teams stay embedded in a problem space, they build profound context, tighter feedback loops, and stronger relationships with users. They don't start from scratch with every new initiative, they evolve and refine based on what they've already learned.

What to watch out for:

- Org charts that mirror outdated tech stacks or political silos
- Overlapping scopes and unclear team boundaries
- PMs juggling unrelated teams with no time for discovery
- Project-based teams that disband before they can build momentum

To move into product mode, you must let structure follow strategy. Organize teams around how your product delivers value, not how your company used to deliver projects. Only then can all the more advanced practices take root.

2. Roles & Responsibilities: Redefining What It Means to Be a Product Manager

Changing the org chart is only the beginning. To truly operate in product mode, we also need to redefine what product roles are, and what they are not. In many organizations, "Product Manager" is still little more than a renamed Project Manager. The title changes, but the expectations stay rooted in coordination, timelines, and stakeholder appeasement. The role becomes more about delivery than about decisions.

In project mode, product managers are often responsible for managing delivery across multiple teams, creating Gantt charts, and checking off feature requests. They are measured by how many items they ship and how well they hit deadlines, not by whether the product created real value. In this model, product managers rarely get the time, context, or authority to think strategically.

In product mode, that changes completely. Product managers are not backlog administrators or passive facilitators. They are decision-makers and outcome owners. They are responsible for understanding the customer, defining value, prioritizing work based on impact, and aligning efforts with product and company strategy. Not only that, but they work in close partnership with design and engineering, what many call the "product trio"[13], to discover and deliver the right solutions.

This shift in responsibility also requires a shift in support. Product managers can only succeed if they are set up to succeed:

- **They need time**. Time for discovery, strategy, and reflection. Spreading a product manager across too many teams or expecting them to constantly chase stakeholder inputs erodes their ability to think deeply and act decisively.
- **They need focus**. Ideally, product managers should work with no more than one or two product teams. This allows them to build context and accountability, and to truly own outcomes.
- **They need authority**. A product manager who is constantly overruled or forced to say "yes" to every request becomes a project manager again. PMs must be empowered to say "no" when ideas don't align with strategy, customer needs, or evidence.

---

[13] This term was originally coined by Teresa Torres

To be clear, not every product manager needs to directly handle strategic tasks like defining the product's positioning or conducting detailed SWOT[14] analyses, this simply isn't a product manager's reality. Many product managers naturally focus more on delivery and managing the numerous day-to-day challenges involved in building and maintaining a successful product. However, the product department as a whole must eventually take ownership of these strategic responsibilities in alignment with the other c-level executives. This means investing strategically in talent development, ensuring that essential know-how, customer understanding, skill sets, and market intelligence are systematically built up over time.

This shift also means changing how performance is measured. Instead of being judged on output and activity, product managers in product mode are evaluated based on learning, impact, and the ability to move key outcomes. This shift takes trust from leadership, collaboration across departments, and a clear shared understanding of what good product management looks like.

Ultimately, moving from project management to product management is not a cosmetic change. It is a fundamental shift in mindset, expectations, and responsibility. And it requires not just a new job description, but a new culture around what product is here to do.

3. Enablement: Autonomy Requires Context

You can't ask teams to make smart decisions without providing them with access to the right information. In project mode, teams are asked to

[14] https://en.wikipedia.org/wiki/SWOT_analysis. Accessed 25.04.2025.

execute. In product mode, they're expected to learn, decide, and adapt. But to accomplish that, they need context, access, and support.

Enablement means giving product teams:

- A clear view of company strategy and business goals
- Direct, ongoing contact with customers, not filtered through intermediaries
- Insight into market trends, competitor behaviour, and emerging technologies
- Outcome-focused success metrics and a shared understanding of what "good" looks like
- The time, psychological safety, and mandate to experiment, learn, and iterate
- Opportunities to visit client sites, attend key sales meetings, and immerse themselves in the realities of their market segment
- A profound understanding of alternative offerings and how the product compares: what makes it stand out and where it needs to improve

Enabling product managers to engage with customers regularly is especially critical. Without direct interaction, it's impossible to deeply understand user problems, validate hypotheses, or prioritize effectively. When PMs are close to real customer needs, discovery becomes faster, decisions become sharper, and products become more relevant.

One of the biggest mistakes is holding teams accountable for outcomes they aren't equipped, or empowered, to influence. If you want them to own value, you must equip them to discover it.

Leadership's Contribution

Leadership must make strategy visible and accessible to all teams, not just as a top-down directive, but as a shared understanding that teams can act on. They need to actively create space for continuous learning by encouraging direct customer interaction. This includes enabling site visits, participation in key sales meetings, and opportunities to shadow support calls, ensuring that product teams are close to customer realities, not shielded from them.

Leaders must also ensure that teams have a strong grasp of their market context. This means understanding the dynamics of their target segments, the strengths, and weaknesses of competitive offerings, and where the product has a clear opportunity to differentiate.

Beyond providing insight, leadership should remove blockers and reduce the noise of random, unstructured requests that derail focus. Their role is to provide clarity and strategic guardrails, while trusting teams to operate autonomously within those boundaries. Most importantly, they must champion a mindset where outcomes, not outputs, define progress.

People and Time: Building Product Capability Is a Process

Equally important is putting the right people into product roles, and recognizing that building a strong product organization is a process, not a switch you can flip. Product management is not a fit for everyone. It demands strategic thinking, customer empathy, structured problem-solving, and strong collaboration skills. Simply renaming project managers isn't enough. Organizations need time, support structures, and intentional guidance to help people grow into these roles. That includes thoughtfully selecting talent, providing structured training and mentorship, and facilitating the mindset shifts required to operate in outcome-driven environments. With the right people and patient support, the organization can evolve into a truly empowered product team.

Best Practice: Clearly Define Roles and Responsibilities

At one of our client organizations, a common pattern emerged: internal stakeholders, often with the best intentions, were still bypassing product management and placing work directly into engineering backlogs.

Despite a shift toward product thinking, legacy behaviours from project mode persisted. The result: engineering teams were overwhelmed, priorities were unclear, and product managers were constantly reacting instead of leading.

In our consultation, we identified that the root issue wasn't ill will, it was role ambiguity. Teams lacked clarity on who was responsible for what, especially in decision-making, prioritization, and stakeholder engagement.

Together with the client, we guided the setup of a Roles and Responsibilities Matrix (RACI)[15] tailored to their product teams. The client took the lead on implementation, engaging product, engineering, design, and business leadership to co-create the matrix. The goal was to

---

15 https://en.wikipedia.org/wiki/Responsibility_assignment_matrix. Accessed 24.04.2025.

make responsibilities transparent across all key roles: product managers, product owners, engineering leads, design leads, and stakeholders.

The RACI clearly defined:

- Who owns product decisions
- Who needs to be consulted (e.g. sales, customer success)
- Where collaboration happens, and where it doesn't
- How engineering requests flow through product

The matrix was rolled out across the organization and supported with internal communication, onboarding updates, and regular reviews.

Adapting the Decision Process

When defining the RACI matrix, it naturally brought the roadmap decision-making process into question. Clearly assigning responsibilities prompted the essential question: are we attending the right meetings where these decisions are made? Consequently, this exercise led us to adapt the decision-making process for the roadmap.

As a result of these changes, the product team regained its role as the primary gateway for new initiatives. Engineering teams were shielded from unfiltered requests, gaining valuable focus. Stakeholders benefited from a transparent and structured process to introduce new ideas without bypassing the product team. Overall, this adaptation marked a significant turning point toward establishing genuine product ownership.

What You Can Do as a Product Leader

✔Audit Your Current Structure
Clearly identify current role definitions and clarify gaps between responsibilities and expectations.

✔Build Cross-Functional Teams
Advocate internally for dedicated teams with clearly defined ownership of outcomes rather than projects.

✔Empower Teams with Clear Boundaries
Establish clear strategic guardrails that allow product teams to make autonomous decisions within defined boundaries. Avoid granting excessive autonomy initially, as too much freedom without sufficient context or alignment can become counterproductive and cause confusion.

✔Align Leadership to Support Teams
Coach senior leaders on the benefits of supporting rather than controlling product teams.

✔ Create Continuous Learning Opportunities
Implement ongoing training, mentorship, and skill-building sessions (i.e. communities of practice, formal training, visiting conference etc.) to reinforce product-centric behaviours and capabilities.

Test Your Own Company

Test your company with the **Project to Product Self-Assessment** by scanning the code or go to: product-masterclass.com/p2passessment

CHALLENGE 6: Push vs. Pull

Push Builds Pressure. Pull Builds Ownership and Clarity.

Why Push vs. Pull Matters to Product Leaders

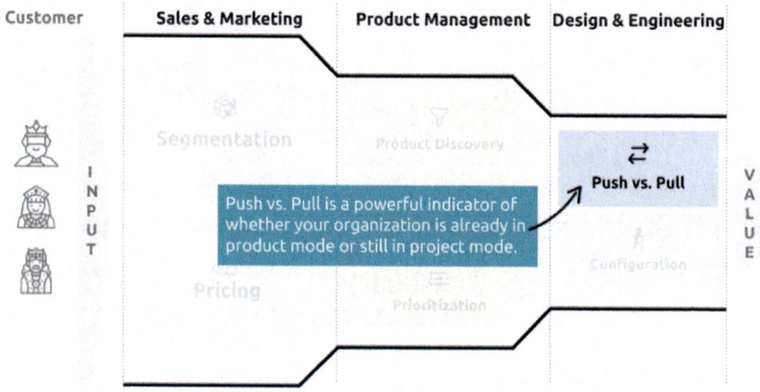

In modern product companies, engineering teams don't wait to be told what to build, they collaborate with a product and UX people to decide what solution to build, and they pull in validated, well-understood work when they're ready. This approach gives teams autonomy, clarity, and a sense of ownership. But in many hybrid or project-driven organizations, the opposite dynamic dominates: work is pushed onto engineering, often unvalidated, underexplored, and under pressure.

That dynamic breaks more than just timelines. It erodes trust, disengages teams, and disconnects product development from actual value. As a Product Leader, your job isn't only to deliver features, it's to create an environment where good decisions can be made upstream, and where teams are empowered to build with purpose, not panic.

The Push Trap

In push environments, the flow of work feels mechanical. Features are defined by stakeholders or project leads, often with rigid scope and firm deadlines. There's little space to ask why. Engineering receives feature specs just before development, with no chance to raise flags, assess trade-offs, or question assumptions.

The predictable result: rework, missed expectations, technical shortcuts, and rising frustration. Engineers feel like order takers. Product feels like a bottleneck. Everyone rushes to deliver, but no one knows if it will matter.

This way of working is regularly mistaken for agility. There are sprints, standups, and boards, but under the surface, it's still waterfall logic in disguise.

What Pull Really Means

Pull mode reverses the traditional dynamic. It assumes that discovery and delivery are distinct yet closely interconnected phases. Product, UX, and engineering continuously explore opportunities together, an approach typically called Continuous Discovery[16]. Problems are validated, and solutions are collaboratively defined. Only once the team has clear confidence in the why, the what, and the how, the work gets pulled into development.

---

[16] Marty Cagan, https://www.svpg.com/dual-track-agile/. Accessed 25.04.2025.

This process fosters alignment and significantly reduces waste. Teams move faster, not because they're under pressure, but because they begin with clarity and a shared commitment. Engineers do more than write code; they actively shape solutions. Product teams don't merely prioritize tasks, they prioritize meaningful outcomes.

Why Push Still Rules in Hybrid Orgs

The pressure to push is especially strong in companies that straddle the line between project mode and product mode. Roadmaps are packed with stakeholder promises. Sales needs commitments. Quarterly plans must be delivered. So the organization defines features up front and throws them over the wall.

There's often no discovery buffer, just a direct handoff from wishful thinking to engineering sprint. When teams inevitably hit problems, the timeline doesn't adjust, the blame just shifts.

In time, engineers stop engaging deeply. They follow instructions. They stop raising risks because no one listened before. Product becomes reactive. Morale erodes. And the whole company continues to run, but no one's steering.

Best Practice: From RACI to Real Pull. How One Company Built a Shaping and Betting Process

The company we mentioned earlier, the one that introduced a RACI matrix to clarify roles and responsibilities, didn't stop there. Once product regained its role as the gateway for new initiatives, they faced the next challenge: how to decide what should actually move into delivery.

Previously, features were simply pushed onto engineering teams as predefined requests: often vague, frequently urgent, and rarely validated. Engineers felt like mere executors, and product managers functioned primarily as translators. Both sides raced toward deadlines, hoping the outcomes would somehow align.

Encouraged by the new spirit in the company, one of the engineering leads raised the question: Could we go further and prevent things from getting pushed into development and last-minute ideas from stakeholders bypassing this process entirely? He suggested borrowing concepts from the Shape Up[17] methodology, in particular the idea of structured betting tables, a system that would create clear decision points, reduce noise, and reinforce shared ownership.

With their newly established RACI structure and the betting tables, product managers and engineering leads seized the opportunity to evolve further by introducing a structured shaping process. Instead of pushing raw ideas directly into development, they collaboratively shaped them beforehand. Product managers contributed profound customer insights and strategic alignment, while engineering provided valuable feasibility perspectives and technical guidance. Their new mantra was clear: nothing entered the backlog unless both sides agreed on the problem definition, potential value, and scope.

---

[17] If you are not familiar with Shape Up, we recommend reading the book Shape Up: Stop Running in Circles and Ship Work that Matters by Ryan Singer https://basecamp.com/shapeup

This shift immediately enhanced team alignment and mutual trust. Engineers finally felt heard, and product managers learned to articulate genuine customer problems clearly rather than presenting mere feature lists.

By integrating shaping and structured betting, this company established a genuine pull system founded on trust, validation, and strategic focus. More importantly, it cultivated a newfound pride among teams, empowering them to make confident decisions based on shared understanding and thoughtful deliberation, rather than urgency or hierarchy.

What You Can Do as a Product Leader

✔Create a Discovery Buffer & Visibility
Don't let engineering start work that hasn't been validated. Introduce a buffer between discovery and delivery and make discovery efforts visible. This gives teams time to validate, before committing to code.

✔Frame Work as Problems, Not Features
Shift conversations with stakeholders from "what do you want built" to "what problem are we solving." This small change reduces scope creep and sets the stage for shared ownership.

✔Build a Strong Product & Engineering Collaboration
Establish regular sessions where product and engineering collaborate on incoming ideas. Discuss feasibility, risks, and alternatives before a ticket is created. This builds mutual respect and better solutions.

✔Allow Teams to Pull Work When Ready

Make it clear that delivery teams are not there to serve deadlines, they're there to deliver outcomes. Make sure to establish a commonly accepted Definition of ready and include measures for success. Encourage teams to commit only to work they understand. Trust builds when teams have control over what they take on.

✔Close the feedback loop

If you write down the expected outcome before implementing things, you should also review the actual outcome to learn and adjust. This will be a valuable learning experience for the whole organization.

The Deeper Shift

Push is about control. It's what happens when leadership is afraid that nothing will get done without pressure.

Pull is about trust. It assumes that when people understand the why and are given the space, they'll do the right thing.

If you want a product company that builds with clarity, confidence, and speed, you have to create a system where teams pull, not one where work is constantly pushed their way. Because real velocity doesn't come from pressure. It comes from alignment.

Test Your Own Company

Test your company with the **Project to Product Self-Assessment** by scanning the code or go to: product-masterclass.com/p2passessment

CHALLENGE 7: Configuration

Decouple Sales Volume from Engineering Effort

Why Configurations Strategy Matters to Product Leaders

As product leaders shift their teams from project mode to product mode, they face a critical challenge: balancing individual customer needs against long-term scalability. In a traditional project mode, tailoring software to each customer's unique demands is straightforward because each implementation stands alone. But when serving multiple customers with a unified product, conflicting requirements emerge and custom-coding each request quickly becomes unsustainable.

Without a thoughtful strategy, product & engineering teams default to short-term fixes, embedding customer-specific exceptions directly into the codebase. Over time, this practice leads to technical debt, complexity, and reduced velocity. Product leaders must proactively invest in configurability and flexible architecture, even though these can temporarily slow down immediate feature delivery.

By prioritizing configurability, leaders lay the groundwork for scalable growth, ensure product stability, and maintain customer satisfaction, without sacrificing their roadmap or drowning their teams in technical chaos.

Configuration Options in Software Development

In software, we aim to model standard use cases for our customer segments in such a way that we create configuration options allowing us, or the customer, to tailor the software to their needs. This variation can be handled in multiple ways. The following classification is commonly used:

Custom Code: The most direct and risky path. Individual customer logic is implemented directly in the product's codebase. In project work, this is standard practice, no configuration is needed because the solution is built exactly to specification. Adjustments are made by rewriting code when the customer's needs change. This works fine for one customer, but becomes a major problem when onboarding a second. Writing exceptions into the product for each new customer causes maintenance costs to explode (see Challenge 2 – Pricing) and puts pressure on development capacity (see Challenge 6 – Push vs. Pull).

Feature Toggles: A partial improvement. Features can be enabled or disabled for individual customers. This is often used in project mode companies to make custom-coded features invisible to others, a practice known as feature gating. The problem? Development and maintenance costs remain the same as for custom code. Just because the feature is hidden doesn't mean it's any less complex. Often the argument is,

"Maybe other customers will want it too." But that's precisely the job of product discovery (Challenge 3), to validate that others truly need it. If a feature only serves one customer, it must be treated as a custom request and priced accordingly (Challenge 2).

(Self-service) Configuration: Ideally, configuration is self-service through interfaces or setup flows. For more complex features, it may require assistance from a rollout or consulting team. Either way, configuration should not require engineers to write new code. Investments here can slow down short-term delivery, but speed up onboarding and reduce support effort in the long run. A good rule of thumb is to aim to cover 80% of typical customer needs through product-side configurations. This is often called a modular product architecture.

External Configuration: Plugins, APIs, Webhooks: This is the most scalable form of variability. Customers, or third-party partners, extend the product using clean interfaces, without touching core code. Plug-in systems shift the burden of implementation to external developers, while APIs and webhooks allow external systems to modify or react to product behaviour. Importantly, this logic must run in a separate environment. Any work done here must be scoped, priced, and maintained separately. Internally, such teams must operate with cost recovery in mind, while product teams stay focused on building for the broader market.

Why Hybrid Organizations Struggle

In hybrid organizations, those transitioning from project to product, this topic is often neglected. There is no clear guideline for what should be configurable and what should not. As a result:

- Individual customer requirements are implemented as one-off solutions.
- No one maintains a clear list of configurations.
- Engineers are unsure which customers use which settings.
- Bugs arise due to unforeseen dependencies between configurations.

The result is regularly a fragile product, high maintenance overhead, and limited ability to evolve the product without fear of breaking existing setups.

Instead, companies should treat feature requests like ideas. Taking the customer seriously, but also assessing the process and requirements with other clients and the broader market. Based on the process variation in the market, the team can decide, if and how, to implement the functionality.

Best Practice: Shopify and Other Platforms

Shopify combines multiple approaches. Core functionality is configurable. More advanced variations is handled through plugins. And if that's not enough, developers can use webhooks or APIs to build their own logic, without modifying Shopify's core product. The external logic is maintained by the customer or third party.

Further Examples

The Chrome browser supports extensions. WordPress allows customization via plugins. Slack offers open APIs. Each of these platforms demonstrates how configurability, when designed well, can support variation without compromising the core product.

Configurability is what enables a product to serve many customers. Without it, variation creates chaos. With it, you can scale.

Best Practice: Map Your Existing Configuration Landscape

One client we worked with struggled with inconsistent behaviours across customers and had no clear overview of what could already be configured in the product.

Before making decisions about their future configuration strategy, the team stepped back and created a structured inventory of all existing customization mechanisms. This proved to be a crucial turning point.

We recommend product teams assess the following areas:

- **Custom Code**: Where is logic hardcoded for individual customers? How much of the codebase contains customer-specific branches or exceptions?
- **Feature Toggles**: Which toggles exist, who uses them, and how many are still needed? Are toggles properly documented and owned?

- **Configuration Files & Settings**: What can be changed by users or rollout teams without writing new code? Are these settings accessible, tested, and scalable?
- **Plugins & Extension Points**: Are there clean, governed ways to extend the product? Are these mechanisms being used consistently?
- **APIs & Webhooks**: Which APIs are used externally, and how are they maintained? Are webhooks reliable and well documented?

The outcome was both surprising and clarifying. Many features were only active for one or two customers. Some configurations weren't known to the teams before. And key decisions about what should or shouldn't be configurable had never been made consciously.

This mapping gave the team a much clearer picture of their current configuration landscape and variation model. It helped them decide which features to deprecate, where to consolidate logic, and which types of variation to support going forward.

It also became a shared reference across product and engineering, bringing clarity to discussions about configurability. Instead of reacting to individual requests, teams could now proactively shape a configuration strategy aligned with the product vision.

Bonus effect: this process can also help uncover segments that can be served in a standardized way, linking directly back to Challenge 1, Segmentation.

What You Can Do as a Product Leader

✔Create and Maintain a Living Configuration Register

The goal with configuration is freeing up capacity in your engineering team. Create a list of all your configurations. Assess the effort in your organization. Try to eliminate the ones which involve your engineers by outsourcing it to customers (API, Plugins) or a configuration interface. Establish review cycles, some toggles are only needed temporarily and should be retired. This keeps your configuration footprint lean and intentional.

✔Define a Configuration Vision

Not every variation is worth supporting. Clarify what your product should support and what it shouldn't. Tie configuration decisions back to customer segmentation: Who are you serving, and which variations truly create scalable value?

✔Validate Before You Build

Treat configuration like a feature. Validate demand before increasing complexity. Ask: who requires this, and why? Use discovery to see how different customers treat the situation.

Building configurability into your product is a double-edged sword, it can unlock scale and be a competitive advantage, or it can bury your teams in complexity. When done reactively, it's just disguised complexity. Your role is to be the steward of scalable variation, ensuring your product adapts without fracturing.

Why This Challenge Reflects All the Others

How you manage configurability shows how aligned your company really is:

- If segmentation is unclear, you won't know what needs to be configurable. The variance is simply too big.
- If pricing doesn't account for complexity, you'll say yes to costly one-offs.
- If your discovery muscle is weak, you'll be likely to build for one customer opposed to a configurable standard.
- If prioritization fails, engineering will build exceptions instead of scalable solutions.

Configurability isn't just a technical concern, it's a mirror of how well you know your segment(s) and what is important and what is not.

If you manage it well, it enables scale. If you ignore it, it silently kills your ability to move.

Test Your Own Company

Test your company with the **Project to Product Self-Assessment** by scanning the code or go to: product-masterclass.com/p2passessment

Final Challenge: Strategy, Culture and Mindset

Connecting the Dots

Why Strategy, Culture, and Mindset Matter to Product Leaders

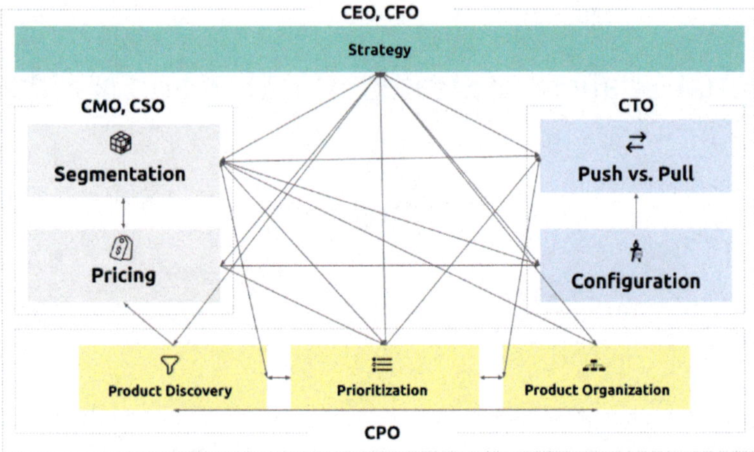

If your company can clearly and consistently answer the seven challenges (segmentation, pricing, product discovery, prioritization, product organization, push vs. pull, and configuration) that is a big part of your product strategy. You don't necessarily need a polished vision deck or a grand positioning statement, although it helps. You need coherent decisions across the organization on what you build, who you build it for, and how you deliver it at scale. Just as importantly, your product strategy must define how those decisions are made, what principles guide them, and who owns them.

But here's the hard part: as a Product Leader, you don't own those decisions alone. To change the strategy, you need to influence people outside your direct responsibility and often above you in the hierarchy. That's why this is the hardest challenge, it's not just structural, it's deeply personal, political, and cultural.

Seven Strategic Guardrails for Everyday Decision-Making

Product strategy isn't just a slide deck, it's the set of trade-offs your organization consistently makes.

These seven questions don't claim to cover every aspect of strategy. But they serve as powerful guiding questions, a practical lens to stress-test your strategy, reveal misalignments, and create guardrails for everyday decision-making:

- Who are we selling to? (Challenge 1: Segmentation)
- What are we charging for and why? How do you treat special requests concerning pricing? (Challenge 2: Pricing)
- How do we decide what to build? (Challenge 3: Product Discovery)
- What do we do first, and what do we ignore? (Challenge 4: Prioritization)
- How do we structure teams and ownership? (Challenge 5: Product Organization)
- How does work flow from idea to release? (Challenge 6: Push vs. Pull)
- How do we scale variation across customers? (Challenge 7: Configuration)

If your organization lacks clear, deliberate answers to these questions, it may not be operating with a coherent product strategy, just a collection of habits and historical decisions. Strategy isn't just what's written down; it's reflected in the trade-offs you consistently make across these dimensions.

The Cultural Gap Between Project and Product Thinking

In a project mode, the logic is simple: say yes, deliver the scope, move to the next deal. It's transactional. The customer defines success.

In product mode, saying yes to everything is the fastest way to fail. You have to focus, say no, and scale through repeatability. That requires a mindset shift across the whole company, not just within the product team.

But here's the catch: while the product team might already be operating in product mode, the rest of the organization often behaves like a project business, and not because they don't "get it". They're responding to the incentive structures and mental models that have historically made them successful.

Leadership is held accountable for revenue targets and timelines, not for scalable architecture or customer outcomes. Finance needs predictable forecasting, so it funds initiatives like projects with fixed scope and delivery dates. Sales is rewarded for closing deals fast, not for aligning with long-term product vision. These are not necessarily dysfunctions, they are just rational responses and design decisions to the way the system is currently operating in a project environment.

That's what makes transformation so hard. It's not about introducing new tools or frameworks, it's about shifting the underlying assumptions and realigning incentives across functions. Until that happens, even well-intentioned teams will fall back into project-mode behaviours because the system rewards them for it.

Why This Is the Result of Every Other Challenge

Every one of the earlier challenges is a reflection of your company's strategic clarity. If your organization struggles to define its focus, make trade-offs, or align on direction, these issues will show up across all seven challenges:

If you don't segment, you'll over-customize.
Without a clear definition of your target customer, every customer feels equally important. The result: exceptions in the code, long onboarding projects, and a product that becomes harder to scale.

If you don't price for complexity, you'll underfund engineering.
Without a pricing model aligned to the effort and value of individual requests, engineering capacity gets drained. Teams end up overloaded, and product progress stalls.

If you don't validate ideas, you'll build the wrong features.
Without a clear problem-solution fit and evidence from your actual users, you'll end up investing time and resources in functionality that doesn't move the needle.

If you don't have strategic clarity in prioritization, you'll try to do everything, or focus on the wrong things.
Without a strategy, there are no shared criteria for what matters most. Prioritization becomes reactive, driven by urgency, influence, or habit, not by impact.

If your team structure isn't aligned to product outcomes, you won't deliver product results.
Product strategy is embedded in how your teams are structured. If your teams are aligned to customers or internal projects instead of market problems, they'll optimize for the wrong things. Long-term ownership and accountability only emerge when teams are empowered to deliver outcomes, not just features.

If you push work into teams, it means the strategy isn't clear enough to pull.
When strategy defines clear goals, empowered teams can decide how to reach them. If work is pushed into teams, it often means there's no clarity on outcomes, so stakeholders try to fill the gap with deliverables.

If you don't manage configurability, it's frequently because you don't know what your product should support.
Without strategic focus, it's tempting to say yes to every edge case. But not every variation deserves a solution. Strategy helps you decide what should be standard, what should be configurable, and what shouldn't exist at all.

What You Can Do as a Product Leader

✔ Use the Seven Challenges as Strategic Guardrails

Treat each challenge not just as a problem to solve, but as a **lens** to frame decisions and align trade-offs. Use them to run a diagnostic on your current state and surface the hidden patterns behind your roadmap chaos, delivery bottlenecks, or incentive misfires. Please don't hesitate to use our self-assessment to get started.

✔ Translate Frustration into Structure

If Sales is pushing complexity, ask: "What are they rewarded for?". If Engineering is stuck in rework, ask: "Where's the entry point for unvalidated ideas?". Every dysfunction in your system is logical if you understand its **incentives**. Your role isn't just to react, it's to trace symptoms back to **structural causes**, then influence change through clarity and persistence

✔ Build a Lighthouse Team That Works Differently

Don't wait for permission to "fix" the company, instead: model the future. Choose one product team, define a clear segment, set up proper discovery, align incentives with impact, and prioritize based on customer outcomes. Then show others the difference it makes in clarity, delivery, and morale.

✔ **Rewire Relationships with Sales, Finance, and Other Leaders**

Sales doesn't need to be "trained", they need to see how product success helps them win better deals. Finance doesn't need a new model, they need confidence in your roadmap, to invest. Treat every stakeholder as a co-owner of outcomes, and focus on what *they* risk or gain when the company fails to scale.

✔ **Use Success Metrics to Shift the System**

Define what success looks like before you ship. Measure what actually happens. And use that gap to introduce strategic tension. Every failed feature is an opportunity to ask: *"How can we avoid wasting effort next time?"* This is your Trojan horse to introduce better discovery, pricing logic, and prioritization

Change won't come from a single meeting. But with clarity, persistence, and empathy, you can start shifting your organization's mindset, one decision at a time.

CHAPTER 3

Leading the Change

In the last chapter we described the recurring patterns, the 7 challenges for projects to produce. In this chapter, we want to give you insights, how we help companies start the change and how you can do it yourself as a product leader.

The Two Reasons Why Change Is Hard

First: You Can't Fix What You Can't See

Shifting from project mode to product mode isn't just a simple process change, it's a complex problem. These kinds of problems are difficult to solve because they involve many moving parts, changing conditions, and incomplete information. There's no single clear definition, no one-size-fits-all solution. Different teams have conflicting goals. Fixing one area often creates issues in another. The situation continues to evolve, and it's difficult to predict the full impact of any change. That's why this kind of transformation requires more than just a new process, it demands a new way of thinking across the entire organization.

Companies frequently misdiagnose their problems by focusing on surface-level symptoms instead of addressing the deeper causes. Take engineering delays, for example: they're typically considered purely an engineering issue, leading to quick fixes like stricter project controls or hiring more developers. But in reality, these delays usually reflect deeper, systemic issues that span the entire organization.

Late deliveries often begin far upstream. They start with promises in the sales process for custom solutions made without fully grasping the complexity involved. Product teams then struggle to prioritize, overwhelmed by a flood of unvalidated stakeholder demands. Meanwhile, marketing targets a broad, unsegmented audience, inviting a wide range of special feature requests that only increase the pressure on engineering and product teams. These aren't isolated issues, they're the real root causes behind what frequently appears to be just an engineering problem.

The real challenge lies in recognizing these deeper connections and seeing how cause and effect play out across departments. How upstream decisions in product, sales, or marketing can create downstream consequences in engineering, product delivery, and ultimately customer value.

Solving such interconnected issues cannot rely on linear or simplistic solutions. Instead, it requires a holistic perspective, one that sees clearly across the entire customer journey and organizational structure. Changes made in one area inevitably affect others, often in unpredictable ways.

Only by embracing the inherent complexity and interconnectedness of these challenges, companies can truly succeed in transitioning sustainably to product mode, delivering real and scalable value to their customers.

It took us many attempts and countless discussions to disentangle the different challenges from one another. Cutting through the noise and identifying the true root causes behind recurring issues was far from straightforward. In the end, this clarity is what enables you to lead the change by making the impact of decisions across the entire company visible and understandable.

Second: The Solution Is Outside Your Product Organization

In most companies, product and engineering feel the pain first. They're the ones who can't keep up. They're the ones working nights and weekends to make the release. So naturally, they're the first to want change.

They start reading and exploring solutions. They learn about empowered product teams, product discovery techniques, outcome-driven roadmaps.

And then... nothing changes.

Because while they're thinking in product mode, the rest of the company still thinks in project mode.

Customer success still promises deliverables. Finance still funds projects. Sales still sell timelines. Stakeholders still expect output. And C-level leadership still wants predictability over progress.

Product and engineering are trying to play a different game, but they're playing on the same field, with a team that's running a different playbook.

That's the part many product leaders would rather not admit. They try to fix things by improving how product management works. Better processes, clearer roles, smarter frameworks. They focus on their realm of responsibility, product management practices. Earlier we referred to this as the egg organization. Product thinks product (yolk) whereas all others still think in project (white).

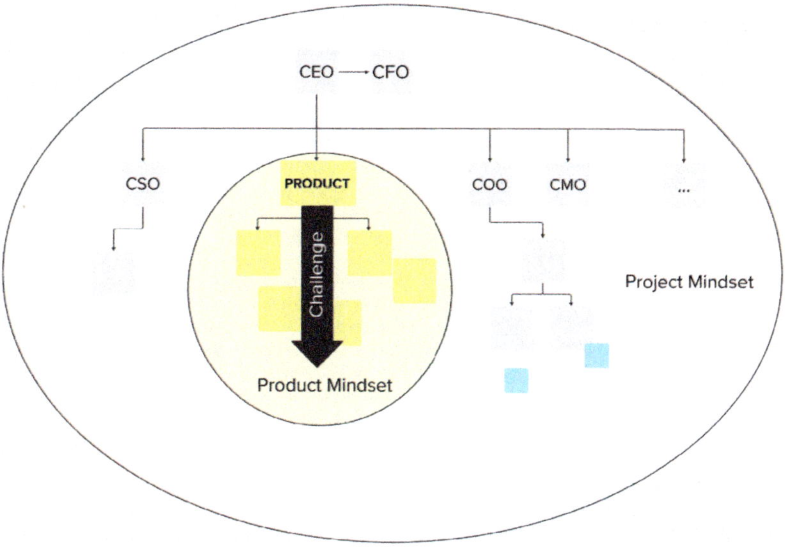

The solution to your struggles is probably not (only) inside your product management team. Although it is important to enable your team, there is an even more important and harder challenge:

Changing the environment your team is operating in.

Real change has to happen outside your product teams at the company level. And this change is harder for you to achieve, since it is beyond your control and realm of responsibility.

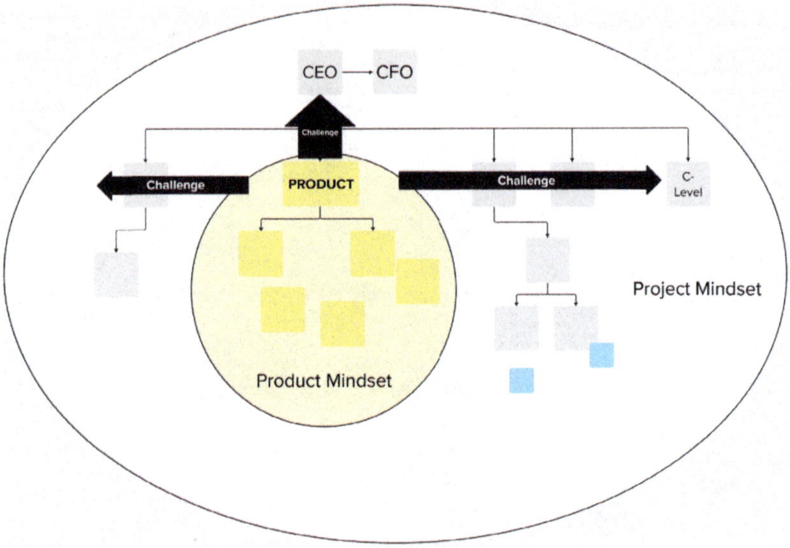

You don't just need better product teams. You need aligned leadership, a shared mindset, and a willingness to start doing things differently across departments. Your common mindset in the leadership team needs to change from delivering projects toward creating products.

Since this change is mostly out of your realm of responsibility and above your hierarchical level, we call that "Level-up". You need to influence the mindset and decisions of people outside your product organisation and hierarchically above you. That imposes a significant challenge for you.

This is the true challenge.

This chapter is about how to create that change, through a structured process that helps the entire organization move, from awareness to alignment, from talking to doing.

4 Steps to Lead the Change

Step 1: Understand Yourself, What's Really Going Wrong. Think Systemically, Not Locally

Context – What We Want to Achieve in This Step

Many product leaders begin their transformation efforts by focusing primarily on their teams. They introduce new structures, train their product managers, and experiment with enhanced planning methods. While these actions are valuable and often necessary, they seldom result in the desired outcome if approached in isolation.

Before driving meaningful organizational transformation, it's essential to identify and understand the deeper, interconnected systemic issues. The aim of this step is to clearly understand these systemic dynamics and recognize the structural incentives and hidden patterns influencing your organization's struggles. This more profound understanding allows you to effectively address root causes, leading to significant and lasting improvements.

The Challenge – Why This Is Hard

As a product leader, you've probably spent most of your time optimizing within your domain, rarely being asked to zoom out and consider how the entire company works together. Perhaps you began your career as a Product Owner focused on delivering great products, later progressing to Senior Product Manager influencing strategy, and eventually becoming a Product Leader with true responsibility for the product's overall success. Throughout your career, you've probably spent most of your time deeply focused on your specific product domain.

This specialized focus often makes it difficult to see the systemic root causes. The transformation from project to product mode is a complex problem, and solving it requires a holistic view of the organization, not a domain-specific lens. Without that, it's easy to misinterpret symptoms like engineering delays, which may actually stem from upstream factors such as leadership expectations, promises to customers, or flawed pricing strategies.

To make things harder, the consequences of these systemic issues usually emerge with a delay, making it even more challenging to trace problems back to their true origins.

How You Can Do It Yourself – Practical Ways to Take Action

Reading this book was a strong first step. Now, make sure you truly understand the seven challenges, and how they reinforce one another. Look closely at your company's data: Which customer segments are you serving? How is your product priced? Are you validating ideas effectively? How are priorities set, and how does engineering actually operate? What's your approach to configuration? Step back and examine how your organization really works.

You can also try to sketch organizational incentives and trade-offs: Visualize the incentive structures across different departments, making hidden relationships explicit. Look specifically at which behaviours are encouraged by current goals, targets, or reward systems.

Finally, use our self-assessment tool to get an objective view of where your company is already strong, and where there's room for improvement.

Test your company with the **Project to Product Self-Assessment** by scanning the code or go to: product-masterclass.com/p2passessment

Taking these steps for yourself will help you clearly understand the systemic dynamics at play, and that clarity is your greatest asset. The better you understand the challenges yourself, the easier it becomes to explain them to others, build alignment, and lead the transformation.

Step 2: Align Leadership. Get Everyone on the Same Page

Context – What We Want to Achieve in This Step

The shift from project to product requires genuine alignment at the leadership level. You need to reprogram the decision processes in your company operating system. Thinking differently about project vs. product, will eventually lead to other decisions for you, and your company. Your common mindset in the leadership team needs to evolve to achieve scalability and growth.

The goal of this step is aligning your leadership team around a unified strategic direction focused on sustainable scalability.

The Challenge – Why This Is Hard

If you want to change how your company makes decisions, you need to influence the people making them. That includes your peers, and often, leaders above you. And if you've ever tried to change just one person's mind, you know how difficult that already is.

Now imagine shifting the mindset of an entire leadership team.

That's why real organizational change is so hard. Each department (sales, finance, marketing, customer success, engineering) sees the world through its lens. What feels urgent to you may not even register as a problem to someone else. And when you show up with a ready-made solution, you typically trigger resistance. No one likes being told how to change, especially by someone outside their function.

It's not personal. People respond to the incentives, beliefs, and success patterns that have worked for them in the past.

We call this the *Company OS*[18]: your organization's mental operating system. It's not the tools or the org chart. It's the mindset, defaults, and decision patterns baked into how your company runs today.

Changing this system means changing how people think. And that's why this work is so difficult, and so important.

How We Do It – Our Experience From the Past

When working with clients, our initial step involves conducting a deep and thorough analysis of the company. We create a comprehensive "X-ray" of the organization, comparing its current state against the "X-ray" of successful product-driven organizations. This comparative analysis helps us pinpoint exactly where to initiate the transition and implement meaningful change.

We typically begin by examining the company's structure and history. Understanding how the organization has evolved provides critical context, as every company is different. For instance, some businesses place product teams under the engineering department, while others integrate engineering into the product organization. Older companies might still refer to engineering and product as 'IT,' reflecting a traditional view of technology as a support function rather than a strategic partner. Some have highly developed customer success teams,

[18] The term Company Operating System (OS) was introduced to us by our Product Masterclass Coach Rasmus Breyer. We kept the term ever since because it is a great metaphor.

while others rely more heavily on traditional service departments or hotlines.

We also analyse how product teams are organized, their formal roles and titles, and how decision-making processes are structured, especially who gets involved and how those decisions are made. Although this list isn't exhaustive, it gives you a strong sense of how we approach our diagnostic work and where we begin to uncover systemic patterns that shape organizational behaviour.

After assessing the current structure, we turn our attention toward the organization's desired future state. While we are usually provided with a high-level vision by our primary contact, often the CEO, gathering more detailed insights is critical. To build a complete 360-degree assessment of the situation, we conduct informal and in-depth conversations with all C-level executives. In these discussions, we explore their specific challenges, their hopes for change, and their perspectives on where the organization should head strategically.

These days, we typically kick off the process with structured questionnaires to lay the groundwork for our conversations. This preparation helps us tailor the discussions and ensures we focus on the most relevant topics. Regardless of whether the insights come from forms, interviews, or informal dialogue, the objective remains the same: to uncover each executive's unique perspective and their ideas for driving meaningful, lasting change.

If the company operates in an unfamiliar industry or deals with specialized processes or technologies, we enhance our research by bringing in external experts with profound domain knowledge. This allows us to quickly build the understanding needed to engage with our clients at eye level, matching the expertise and credibility they're accustomed to from peers within their organization.

All of this preparation culminates in a structured workshop where we bring the entire leadership team together. In this setting, our goal is to introduce and reinforce new thinking patterns that help shift the leadership mindset, from managing individual functions in isolation to collectively enabling the organization's transition toward a scalable, product-driven company.

What Doesn't Work

One thing is clear: what doesn't work is walking into the room and telling everyone else what they need to do. Saying, "Here's what you need to change," rarely lands well, and most likely it won't work for you either. Showing up with a fixed solution and expecting others to follow it will almost always lead to resistance.

Unless you help change the perspectives and thinking patterns of the people involved, it's unrealistic to expect future decisions to be any different. No matter how valid your argument may be, if your approach implies, "I know better," you'll shut down the conversation before it even begins. No one likes being told how to do their job, especially by someone who doesn't work in their area.

What Does Work

We approach the situation differently. Over time, we've found that the most effective way to create alignment is to begin by focusing on the overarching goal shared by everyone in the organization. Rather than starting with what's broken, we start with what the company is trying to achieve. In almost every case, transitioning to product mode includes a desire to become more scalable, and by extension, more profitable. This ambition may come in different forms or under different labels, but some version of it is always present. Otherwise, there would be no reason to move away from the project model.

That shared ambition, scaling sustainably, is not just a product goal, it's a business goal. It speaks to efficiency, clarity, and long-term growth. And importantly, it opens the door to true cross-functional collaboration. When leadership teams unite around this purpose, they become far more open to discussing what needs to change to achieve it.

It creates a shift in the conversation: Not "who's doing it wrong," but "what needs to change so we can scale better?" This is where alignment begins, not in assigning blame, but in jointly identifying friction and opportunity.

After our research phase, we typically run a workshop with the full leadership team. In this workshop, we usually begin by sharing the work we've done in advance to collect and analyse data about the organization. We explain that we've created an "X-ray" of the company, an assessment of its current state, and compared it to patterns in successful product organizations.

This is, in fact, how we developed the model of the seven challenges. These seven areas consistently represent the key differences between project-oriented and product-oriented organizations.

At this point in the workshop, we present a tailored version of the seven challenges based on what we've observed in their organization. Every company is unique, so while most challenges apply in some form, there are often variations or additional aspects that emerge. Still, the seven challenges provide a consistent and proven framework that we use to anchor the conversation and spark meaningful reflection.

We typically walk through each of the seven challenges together with the leadership team, inviting open discussion along the way. It is essential that everyone in the room fully understands what each challenge means in the context of their organization. More importantly, we explore the trade-offs, implications, and interdependencies between the challenges.

Take configuration, for example. Many leaders agree that it would be ideal for customers to be able to fully configure the product themselves. But what does that actually require? It places a heavy burden on engineering, demanding significant time and resources that could otherwise be allocated elsewhere. This leads to a deeper set of questions: Is there enough market demand to justify that investment? Are customers willing to pay for this level of configurability? Can we reliably assess this through product discovery? Do we have the people and skills in place to run such assessments effectively? And what does that decision mean for other functions? If we invest in configuration, how will that affect the sales strategy, the target segments, or the prioritization of other features on the roadmap?

It's all interconnected. Recognizing these connections, and the tradeoffs which come with it is one of the most important outcomes of this conversation.

We really take time for this step. Understanding the challenges between project mode and product mode, and the implication and connection between the challenges, is key to starting the change.

The next step in the process is ranking the challenges. You'll find more details on this in step 3.

How You Can Do It Yourself – Practical Ways to Take Action

In a conversation with a client during a cultural transformation program, we reflected on the progress made. At one point, the client asked, "How do you eat an elephant?" I looked puzzled, and he smiled and said, "Bit by bit." That phrase stuck with me. It's a powerful reminder: real transformation happens step by step, decision by decision.

When we support companies through change, we benefit from two key advantages compared to someone working inside the organization. First, as external advisors, it's often easier for us to be heard. Our outsider perspective brings neutrality, which helps us bypass internal politics and emotional barriers.

Second, we bring experience from guiding many organizations through similar transformations. Experience is what you get right after you need it.[19] We've seen patterns repeat themselves and have developed a clear understanding of the common pitfalls. Thanks to that repeated exposure, we're able to help teams understand the interdependencies of

---

[19] The Art of Shralpinism: Lessons from the Mountains, Jeremy Jones https://www.amazon.de/Art-Shralpinism-Lessons-Mountains/dp/1680513303

the seven challenges before costly mistakes occur. This allows us to guide leadership teams through complexity with clarity and confidence.

Despite those advantages, there is still a great deal you can do as a product leader to shape your company's trajectory. Bit by bit, you can help shift the mindset within your leadership team by spreading knowledge about the difference between project and product thinking, and what that means for the decisions your company makes.

Just as we focus on education in our workshops, you can start internally by sparking conversations. Hand your copy of this book to a colleague with a few notes and ask for their thoughts. Or share a 30-minute conference talk we've given on this topic to build curiosity and interest:

Watch the Keynote: Productized — From Project to Product by scanning the code or go to: https://product-masterclass.com/p2p-book#keynote

You can also actively involve your leadership colleagues in a discussion about how to improve. Companies in transition often operate under high stress. Product isn't delivering, engineering is too slow, marketing feels misaligned. Use these tensions as entry points. Invite your colleagues to reflect on how the company operates. Frame it with their needs in mind: "We'd like to assess our current ways of working so we can help you [insert key frustration here]."

For sales, this might be delivering faster. For marketing, better alignment and messaging. For engineering, more stable sprints. Start with their pain points. Ask them what goals they're aiming for. Then explore how structural changes might help, not just your function, but the company as a whole.

To support this, we created a Project to Product Scorecard, which allows you to replicate our workshop on your own. You can download it for free here:

Download the free Project to Product Scorecard by scanning the code or go to: https://product-masterclass.com/p2p-book#scorecard

The scorecard is essentially a printed version of our Project to Product Assessment. It's designed to help leadership teams evaluate where they are, compare perspectives, and foster productive discussions grounded in shared goals.

Ultimately, these tools are about spreading awareness and creating space for reflection among your leadership team. Help them see how their work is interconnected and how decisions affect the company's ability to scale.

At some point, you'll need to bring everyone together around one table to make real decisions. These early steps are what prepare the ground, so that when the time comes, you're not just having a discussion, but creating true alignment.

These are some ideas, how you can spread the knowledge in your organization and align leadership. The goal should be clear by now, but there are many ways to achieve this goal. Depending on your organization, your culture, your situation, you might come up with other ideas, how to achieve alignment in your company.

Step 3: Rank What Matters Most. You Can't Fix Everything at Once

Context – What We Want To Achieve in This Step

Once we establish a shared understanding of the current challenges and a collective ambition to scale, the next essential step is to focus. In Step 2, we explored how recognizing the systemic issues between project and product mode sets the foundation for transformation.

Just because everyone understands the challenges, as discussed in the previous step, doesn't automatically mean there's alignment on what to do next. We need to create clarity, focus, and a shared commitment to action.

This step is about identifying which challenges to tackle first, and establishing the focus required to make real progress. Without prioritization, all challenges compete equally for attention, leading to stalled initiatives, decision fatigue, and a lack of coordinated progress. Teams become overwhelmed, unsure where to begin, and hesitant to commit.

Prioritization is not just about deciding what to do first, it's about creating clarity, aligning resources, and building the momentum needed to move forward with purpose. By selecting the top areas to work on, we give direction to the change process, build confidence through early wins, and enable coordinated action across teams.

The Challenge – Why This Is Hard

Ranking the seven challenges by importance isn't just a workshop exercise, it's the moment where alignment gets tested. Different departments come with their perspectives, incentives, and urgencies. That's why ranking them can quickly become political. What seems like a neutral list on a whiteboard often hides deeply rooted tensions, competing goals, and trade-offs that few are ready to confront.

Companies transitioning from project to product mode carry legacy habits: saying yes to everything, chasing short-term revenue, and reacting to the loudest voice in the room. These habits make it hard to focus and even harder to say no. Prior commitments, personal investments, and historical success patterns often create resistance to change, even when the current way of working is no longer sustainable.

It's one thing to agree in theory that "we should focus more on one customer segment." (Challenge 1: Segmentation). It's another to turn down a €7 million project because it doesn't fit that segment, something one of our clients had the courage to do. That's not just an operational shift. That's a bold management decision with real consequences.

And that's precisely what makes this step so critical. The point of ranking the challenges isn't just to create a list, it's to create a path forward. It's about building shared conviction around the company's most important goals and being willing to sacrifice lower priorities in service of the bigger picture.

How We Do It – Our Experience From the Past

We ask each participant to rank the seven challenges individually. This exercise prompts them to reflect on the impact of each challenge from the perspective of their unique role and responsibilities. Naturally, the results vary. Each leader brings a different lens shaped by their department, experience, and strategic priorities.

We then display these individual rankings on a whiteboard, whether digital or physical, so that everyone can see the variety of viewpoints across the leadership team. The real value, however, lies in the discussion that follows: a dialogue where participants openly explain their reasoning, explore trade-offs, and raise concerns.

We do not rely on a mathematical formula or weighting system to determine which challenges matter most. The value is in the conversation, the back-and-forth exchange of perspectives that leads to more profound understanding.

If one challenge ranks high across most participants, it naturally becomes a candidate for prioritization. But we also make it a point to hear from participants who did not rank that challenge highly. Their opposing views often bring valuable nuance.

We also pay special attention to outliers. Challenges that were ranked highly by only one or two people. We invite those individuals to share their thinking, which can uncover overlooked but important insights.

Participants are encouraged to revisit and adjust their rankings based on the discussion and arguments presented. Through this open and reflective process, the group typically converges on three top challenges that everyone agrees are critical and is willing to commit to addressing.

This approach creates the space for alignment to form naturally, through honest dialogue and shared conviction, rather than through forced consensus.

How You Can Do It Yourself – Practical Ways to Take Action

If you're leading this process internally, expect it to take more time than when facilitated by an external coach. That's completely normal. Prioritizing systemic change requires space for reflection, alignment, and discussion.

Most importantly, don't rush into solutions. Focus first on building alignment within your leadership team. Real change will come from shared understanding, not from quickly fixing surface-level issues.

This step will take effort, patience, and a willingness to grow together over time. Here are some suggestions to help you move forward:

- **Use the Project-to-Product Scorecard as your guide:** Invite your leadership team to a workshop modelled after the one we describe in this book. The Scorecard, introduced in Step 2, outlines the necessary steps and includes a dedicated section for group discussion and reflection.
- **Start small and build momentum:** Instead of aligning everyone at once, begin with someone who already shares your perspective or shows interest in this transformation. Review the challenges together, refine your thoughts, and discuss how

these ideas apply to your organization. Once you're aligned, gradually bring others into the conversation.

- **Connect the dots during ongoing meetings:** Even outside formal workshops, use regular leadership meetings to highlight interdependencies between decisions. Help your colleagues see how challenges are connected and how short-term choices affect long-term scalability.
- **Create visible feedback loops:** Document the key outcomes and agreements from your conversations and revisit them frequently. This reinforces shared understanding and helps the team track its progress.
- **Give change time to grow:** Not every shift happens in the first session. Sometimes, all you need to do is plant a seed and let it develop. Stay patient, consistent, and reflective.

If you keep showing up with clarity and curiosity, the shift from scattered opinions to shared priorities will come.

Step 4: Enable Your People to Work Differently

Context – What We Want to Achieve in This Step

Once the leadership team has aligned around strategic priorities, the next essential step is enabling your teams to put these priorities into practice. Transformation isn't just about setting goals, it's about supporting new ways of working and embedding new behaviours within your organization. This step is about equipping people practically, culturally, and operationally, ensuring that your teams are empowered and capable of working effectively in a product-driven environment. The change will take time and is not done in a couple of weeks. The goal in this step is to develop a clear plan for the company, how the change will happen, and assign ownership.

The Challenge – Why This Is Hard

The challenge in this phase lies in translating strategic decisions into concrete, everyday behaviour. While leadership may have agreed on priorities, those decisions need to be broken down, communicated clearly, and made actionable at the team level. This means explaining not just what was decided, but why, and what it means for how teams should work moving forward.

Shifting from project-mode to product-mode is not only about changing tools or processes; it's about helping people adopt a new way of thinking. That requires letting go of legacy habits, rethinking how work is planned and delivered, and creating clarity on what success looks like in a product organization. Without clear guidance and support, teams often default to what they've always done, even if it no longer fits the new direction.

How We Do It – Our Experience From the Past

We specialize in running short, high-impact engagements that bring clarity and momentum to organizations. The process we follow is not about long, drawn-out engagements where we stay onsite endlessly. Our approach is simple: diagnose the core issues, define the right treatment, and hand over a clear path forward.

At this stage, our focus is to help the leadership team take the three most important challenges identified in the previous step and break them down into actionable plans. We work with stakeholders to clarify what exactly needs to change, outline the first steps, and, crucially, assign ownership.

We don't aim to solve everything ourselves. We excel at enabling product organizations through formats like the Product Masterclass. But when it comes to other departments such as sales or marketing, we recognize that our role is to help define the change, not to deliver it ourselves.

What matters most here is accountability. Each key initiative should have a clear owner, a defined outcome, and visible commitment to drive it forward. That's how real change begins.

How You Can Do It Yourself – Practical Ways to Take Action

Once your leadership team is aligned on what needs to change, the next step is to bring those decisions to life. Start by clearly breaking down the priorities into concrete actions and assign responsibilities. Make sure every initiative has a clear owner who is accountable for moving it forward. These owners can be internal champions with influence, or external consultants and partners who bring in needed expertise.

To support implementation, establish a system of ongoing coaching and guidance. Pair team members with experienced mentors inside the company or bring in outside coaches who can reinforce new behaviours, provide feedback, and help resolve obstacles as they arise.

Lastly, build a structure that reinforces accountability. Use transparent success metrics, regular check-ins, and structured retrospectives to measure progress. This not only helps keep momentum but creates a feedback loop that drives continuous learning and adaptation.

The goal is to make the change visible, owned, and supported, so it doesn't remain a strategic intention, but becomes part of how the organization actually operates

CHAPTER 4

The Most Common Misconceptions in the Transformation From Project to Product

Transforming from project mode to product mode is difficult. The journey is full of ambiguity, complexity, and setbacks.

In this chapter, we highlight some of the most common misconceptions we've seen in practice. Wrong assumptions that seem logical on the surface but quietly sabotage progress behind the scenes.

These are the patterns that show up most frequently in organizations making the shift. But they're not exhaustive. Every company brings its own history, incentives, and internal dynamics into the transformation. Think of these misconceptions as a starting point for reflection, not an exhaustive list.

Misconception #1: "This Book Seems to Describe a Waterfall Process. We Want an Agile Process with Iterations"

Agile has been around for over 25 years, and yet, many companies still struggle to make it work. Why? Because they have an "egg" organization: Product and engineering think in products, everybody else thinks in projects. That is the status quo out there, in most companies and the root cause, why Agile is not working.

Scrum and Agile was born in software. And in most organizations, that's where it stayed. Product and engineering teams adopt fancy frameworks, while the rest of the company, operations, marketing, sales, finance, support, etc., hand over feature requests and ask "when can I have it"? They think in projects. The result? An "egg organization" as described above. A product minded core surrounded by a project mindset.

Product people go to conferences, listen to best practices and want to work like Marty Cagan describes product management. In the real world, they get handed over mini projects with timelines and wonder why it does not work the way they heard it at the conference. They put pseudo discoveries on top or deliver the project in "scrum" iterations. Well, thanks, that does not help at all.

You need to start seeing the whole organization, that's the hardest part of what we describe in this book. Think about it: we've written a product management book, but at least half of it isn't about product management at all. Why? Because that's where most teams struggle. The real problems often lie outside the product function. So that's where your transformation has to start.

Misconception #2: "We Can Continue Selling Customization and Still Operate as a Product Company"

Many organizations mistakenly believe they can continue selling heavily customized solutions while transitioning into a scalable product business. This misconception arises from a fear of losing large clients, revenue streams, or sales momentum during the transition. Companies regularly assume they can manage both customized services and standardized products simultaneously without significant drawbacks.

This misconception fundamentally undermines the essence of product scalability: standardization. Customization introduces complexity, fragmenting the codebase and exponentially increasing technical debt. Engineering teams become overwhelmed by constant firefighting, and product teams lose focus, leading to diminished innovation, slower delivery cycles, and ultimately compromised product quality and user experience.

Recently, we had a call with a CPO that illustrated exactly this misconception. He was approached by their CEO, who announced a significant deal involving considerable monthly recurring revenue (MRR). However, this deal required building a custom feature specifically tailored to the client's request. During a detailed walkthrough of their sales process, he reported: "Customer success management is structured as a profit centre, billing their efforts with a 40% margin. Meanwhile, product and engineering teams quote based on anticipated effort. Because these estimates typically result in prices too high for customers to accept, the company often resorts to offering discounted package prices." This scenario is illustrative but quite common in project mode. Consequently, engineering resources quickly become consumed by custom features, leaving limited room for scalable product innovation and slowing overall product development. In this case, the company used 60% of its engineering capacity on maintenance and bug fixing, 30% on custom features, and only 10% on product innovation. Clearly, this approach is unsustainable in the long run.

Obviously, the organization and its leadership team did not fully understand the trade-offs they were committing to and their implications. Start here to find alignment on the leadership level.

Misconception #3: "They Hired Me to Do the Change"

Many product leaders believe that since they've been hired to drive transformation, they are not allowed to bring in additional expertise. You are hired, that the change is happening, does not mean, you are doing it yourself.

Think of yourself as the conductor of an orchestra. You need to read the notes, be able to play, but your job isn't to play every instrument but to guide and coordinate musicians, ensuring harmony and rhythm throughout the performance. Similarly, your role in transformation is to orchestrate, delegate, and ensure every member of your team plays their part effectively.

You are hired to deliver the result. Use the tools and tactics, which lead you there in the fastest and most effective way possible.

Pick your battles and decide who's best equipped to fight them. As a product leader, you need to set the stage that your team can effectively work in product mode, tackling the challenges 3 discovery, 4 prioritization and 5 creating a product org. All other challenges go beyond your area of control.

It is not in your power to tell your CEO, your CSO, or CMO or other C-Level executive what to do. And you will get a serious pushback, if you want to change your organization. You need allies to do that. But remember, you don't need to do everything yourself. Hire or delegate when:

- You face recurring pushback or organizational resistance. Bring in a neutral facilitator or product expert, who has done such a transformation.
- You need speed and specific expertise (e.g. pricing strategy, or operating model, strategic alignment...).
- You want to avoid the politics or emotional toll of being the 'bad cop', bring in somebody to deliver the bad news.
- The company requires fresh perspective or industry benchmarks of how successful product organizations operate.

In short, own the change, but don't carry it alone. Look for somebody who has done such a change in the past. It will save you and your organization time, and therefore money, but even more important, save you from burn out, reduce stress on all sides and increase the chance of success. Successful change leaders don't do it all, they orchestrate effectively.

Misconception #4: "The Stakeholder Is the Customer"

In internal tools or B2B platforms, it's easy to confuse internal stakeholders like department heads or the CEO with a real customer. You build what they request, deliver on their timeline, and assume success.

But stakeholders are not end customers or end users. They come with their own goals, incentives, and political pressures. Building what stakeholders want can feel like progress, but it often means missing what customers actually need.

This is especially true in large, global organizations. We recently worked with a corporate team responsible for a globally used app from a world known brand. Despite their scale and scope, the product team had no direct connection to the end customer. Their roadmap was driven entirely by feature requests from regional sales teams, distribution units, and various internal departments operating within a complex matrix organization. No one in the product team was talking to the users or customers.

This kind of setup can feel productive: plenty of meetings, long roadmaps, aligned stakeholders, but it's not product mode. They essentially act as a delivery agency within the organization.

Product managers must stay connected to actual usage, customer interviews, and outcomes. If not, you are just doing project work, organizing the delivery. That is totally acceptable too. But let's not confuse it with product management.

CONCLUSION

From Clarity to Change

We hope this book has helped you see your organization more clearly.

The challenges you face are rarely just about product management. They're systemic. They're cultural. And often, they're deeply embedded in your company's core business model, in how value is created, how revenue is earned, and what behaviours that model rewards.

Throughout this book, we've shared a mental model to help you diagnose and address these challenges. Our goal was to connect the dots between things that often seem unrelated, but in reality, are tightly linked.

You've now seen the seven core challenges that hold organizations back and how they reinforce each other. You've explored why change is hard, what makes it work, and how to start the shift. And you've got a step-by-step approach to begin the journey.

But more than anything, we hope this book gave you language. Because language creates clarity, and clarity creates movement.

Use what you've learned to spark conversations, challenge assumptions, and reshape how decisions are made. Whether you're a CPO, a VP, or a senior product manager, your role isn't just to manage teams and products, it's to help your company grow into the kind of organization that can truly scale.

This transformation isn't easy. It won't happen overnight. But it is possible. And it starts with people like you.

Let's make the shift from project mode to product mode.
One conversation. One decision. One team at a time.

Further Resources

Watch the Keynote on the book

We gave a talk about the book at the justproduct.de conference. It is filled with illustrative stories and fun to watch. This talk is also great to share with your colleagues to start the conversation about a shift from project to product. Check it out at: https://product-masterclass.com/p2p-book#keynote

Take the Project to Product Self-Assessment

We strongly recommend that you test your organization with the Project to Product Self-Assessment. This will give you a great reference point of where you stand and can help start a discussion with unbiased data rather than opinion: product-masterclass.com/p2passessment

Join the Product Masterclass

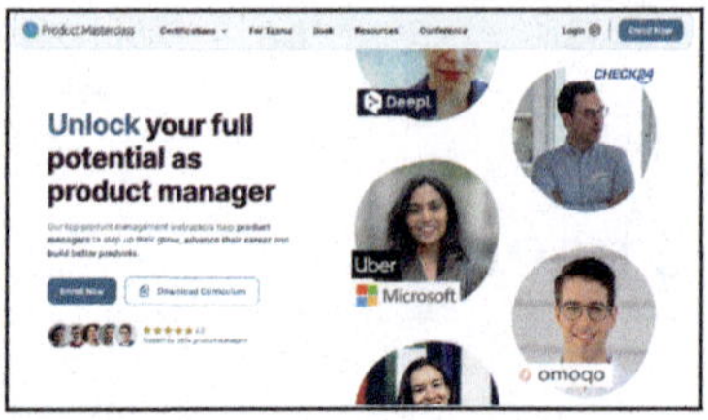

The Product Masterclass is an 8-week coaching on the job to help you and your team adopt a product mindset. It is perfectly suited to enable individuals and product teams to advance their effectiveness in building successful products. For details, check out product-masterclass.com

Project to Product Scorecard

The Product Scorecard will help you facilitate the process in your own company. Download the Scorecard and run the process with your leadership collegues.

Project to Product: Coaching for Leaders

Moving from project to product mode isn't just about product teams, it's about changing how the whole company works. Our coaching gives you personal guidance on how to lead that change: how to build trust, align leadership, and push through resistance when it counts. For details, check out:
product-masterclass.com/p2p-coaching

Thank You

We thought writing a book would be easier. Honestly, if we had known at the outset that this would become a 2.5-year journey, we might not have dared to start. But here we are, and we're proud we did.

We approached this book the same way we build great products: through iteration. The first version was, frankly, terrible. It missed the mark completely. But instead of giving up, we kept refining, revising, and learning. What you're reading now is the 19th iteration of *From Project to Product Mode*.

If we've managed to hit the mark this time, it's not due to our brilliance. Far from it! This book has greatly benefited from the insights, sharp feedback, and constructive criticism of many exceptional product people along the way.

Our deepest gratitude goes out to all who took the time to share their thoughts, ideas, and feedback. Special thanks go to Stefanie Bergfeld, Anna Simon, Sebastian Hohnert, Andreas Hartmann, Jan Kiekeben, Reimar Hantke, Jakub Müller, Dominik Rupprecht, Benjamin Schmid, Natalie Moschner, Christoph Gomez, Matthias Maar, Jono Jacobs, Simon Leipold, Francesca Negri Smedberg, Thorben Krieger, Bethan Ashley, Michael Schölkopf, Rakibul, Marc Charron, and many others.

If you have contributed but don't see your name here, please forgive our oversight and reach out so we can include you in future editions.

A special thanks go to Michael Muckel. He was the one person who gave us the most valuable feedback a book author can imagine. He nailed it every time, and it sometimes took us months to figure out what he meant and how we can change accordingly. Thank you, Michael!

A special thanks go out to our very first client who undertook a full transformation from project mode to product mode: **André Käber**, at that time CEO of **leogistics GmbH**. We're still deeply impressed by the organization André managed to create. It was only because everyone at logistics openly shared their thoughts with a common goal in mind, that we were able to clearly recognize the seven core challenges. Ever since, we've found these same challenges at the heart of every company we've worked with.

Finally, we sincerely thank **you** for reading this book. Your feedback matters deeply to us, so please don't hesitate to share your thoughts, whether you loved it or think we could do better.

We're just humans trying our best to share what we've learned.

Sincerely,

Thomas Hartmann & Sebastian Borggrewe

About the Authors

Sebastian Borggrewe and Thomas Hartmann created the Product Masterclass to help product managers elevate their skills and build better products.

What started as a program for individuals quickly attracted the attention of companies looking to uplevel their entire teams and shift toward stronger product practices. Over the years, Sebastian and Thomas have seen numerous transformations, helping organizations move from project-based work to true product thinking. Along the way, clear patterns emerged. This book is grounded in those real-world experiences. They are also the founders of the Just Product Conference, one of Europe's largest hybrid product conferences, with over 3,000 participants from around the world.

Imprint

Version 1.0

Publisher: Product Masterclass GmbH

Cover design made by: Julia Comarú Fonseca

www.product-masterclass.com

Printing and distribution on behalf of:
Product Masterclass GmbH, Pariserstraße 14, 81669 Munich, Germany

Printed in Dunstable, United Kingdom

70458704R00097